MW00454626

Through the Maze of Motherhood

of Motherhood

Empowered Mothers Speak

Through the Maze of Motherhood
Empowered Mothers Speak

Erika Horwitz

DEMETER

DEMETER PRESS

Copyright © 2011 Demeter Press

Individual copyright to their work is retained by the authors. All rights reserved. No part of this book may be reproduced or transmitted in any form by any means without permission in writing from the publisher.

Published by:
Demeter Press
c/o Motherhood Initiative for Research and
 Community Involvement (MIRCI)
140 Holland St. West, P.O. 13022
Bradford, ON, L3Z 2Y5
Telephone: 905.775.9089
Email: info@demeterpress.org
Website: www.demeterpress.org

Demeter Press logo based on Skulptur "Demeter" by Maria-Luise Bodirsky
<www.keramik-atelier.bodirsky.edu>

Cover Design: Lakeshia Wheeler
Interior Design: Luciana Ricciutelli

Printed and Bound in Canada

Library and Archives Canada Cataloguing in Publication

Horwitz, Erika, 1961-
        Through the maze of motherhood : empowered mothers speak / Erika Horwitz.

Includes bibliographical references.
ISBN 978-0-9866671-4-5

        1. Motherhood—Social aspects. 2. Motherhood—Psychological aspects. I. Title.

HQ759.H769 2011   306.874'3   C2011-907548-2

To Bonnie,
who "mothered" me through the journey.

And to my Mom, Leila,
whose arms have always been available.

Table of Contents

Acknowledgements

I want to thank Dr. Bonnie Long. She offered her time to read the manuscript several times resulting in supportive feedback, encouragement, and a much needed ear during the many times I found myself struggling. She was a "mother" of sorts, who offered unconditional support and encouragement. Words cannot make justice to how truly grateful I am for her kindness and her belief in me. It is to her that I dedicate this book.

I am deeply grateful to the 15 women who offered their time and shared their narratives with me. This book honours their stories and hopes that their kindness pays forward many fold.

I also want to thank Doctors Judith Daniluk and Jack Martin who along with Bonnie supervised the original study. Their wisdom, encouragement, and expertise were invaluable in the process of conducting, analyzing, and writing up the study. I want to thank Dr. Andrea O'Reilly for her belief in my work and her encouragement along the way. In finalizing the manuscript, Jessica Peart jumped in to help with editorial support on short notice. Her insights and suggestions were invaluable.

I want to express my gratitude to my dear friend Tammy Black-well, who showed up in my life and offered me a dream friendship. She offered an ear, hugs, tea, or whatever I needed. She provided me with support, love, kindness, and encouragement during very difficult personal times while I was working on the book. She gave me hope and renewed my belief in the power of friendship.

I want to thank my girls, Stephanie and Leigh-Ann for putting up with me when I was "psycho" mom (as they called me), and for always giving me a chance to come back to myself. I adore them!

And my sister and oldest friend, Marisa; I am so grateful for her ongoing, unconditional, loving presence in my life since we were children. She has always offered encouragement, love, and connection for most of my life. She is wind beneath my wings.

And to my brother Jaime, who has shown me so much love and care since we were little children, I want to say, life would never be the same without you. Thank you for being such a caring presence during so many times in my life. I adore you!

I want to thank my husband, partner, and companion, Humberto, for always believing in me and my abilities. He travelled this journey of hope, frustration, excitement, hard work, confusion, and joy with patience, empathy, encouragement, humour, and the best of friendships. He is my rock.

Lastly, I want to mention my mother, Leila. She has loved me unconditionally, has always been there when I needed her, and has been a second mother to my daughters. I am grateful for her and know how lucky I am to have had such an amazing mother. I also dedicate this book to her.

Introduction

The Journey

My children cause me the most exquisite suffering of which I have any experience. It is the suffering of ambivalence: the murderous alternation between bitter resentment and raw-edged nerves, and blissful gratification and tenderness.
—Adrienne Rich, *Of Woman Born*

WHEN I WAS TEN YEARS OLD and growing up in Mexico City, I had a dream one night. In my dream I was ten years old and I was expecting a baby; at the time I did not know how babies were made, all I knew was that they grew in the mother's womb. In the dream, I was wearing a green dress that my mom had made for me and I could feel life growing inside me. I remember waking up in the warmth of my bed, savoring every detail of the dream. Those wonderful feelings of being a mother and loving a child of my own stayed with me throughout the day! Thirty-nine years have passed and I now have two daughters, Stephanie, 26, and Leigh-Ann, 22.

My journey as a mother has occurred alongside my journey as a scholar, therapist, parent educator, and researcher in the area of parenting, and in particular mothering. I had my first daughter when I was 23. I had finished my third semester of a Bachelor of Arts in Psychology and been married for three years to my first husband whom I had met when I was 19. Stephanie was the love of my life. I had finally become a mother to a beautiful baby. I was going to be the best mom in the world. I had great plans. I was

1

going to read about development and learn how to feed, nurture, and raise her to be a wonderful human being. I promised not to make the same "mistakes" my parents made. I wanted to respect her, to teach her all that she needed to know. I vowed to communicate well with her and to meet all her needs. I was committed to being patient and fair in all my interactions with her. I was going to have the strongest bond a mother and daughter had ever seen! Oh yeah, I was going to be the mother of the century!

And then reality set in. How can she cry and cry? Why can't I stop her? I'm breastfeeding her, loving her, and only an arm's length away. Why is she crying? Why do I feel so tired? When is she going to stop crying? Where did my freedom go? Why don't I feel excited all the time? I adore her; she is the sweetest creature in the planet. Why is she making it so difficult? These are many of the painful and confusing thoughts I had only two or three weeks after becoming a mother. I experienced the equally powerful feelings of love and devotion while at the same time I felt angry, tired, and ambivalent about the lack of freedom, the sleepless nights, and my baby's non-stop crying during dinner and for hours in the middle of night.

But I had no map to help me navigate these strong emotions, so I quickly pushed them aside because I *loved* this baby and I didn't think these negative feelings belonged with the experience of being a mother. From that moment on and for many years, I focused on a quest to be the best mother in the world. I read books on child development, focused my degree on developmental psychology, and took parenting classes that taught me to be empathic and the "adult" when interacting with my daughter. I read to her, spent lots of time with her, chose my university schedule around her needs, studied with her by my side, and was extremely patient. I even went to therapy to heal my past so that I would not "pass it on" to her. As if that was not enough, I did not allow her dad to act in ways that I thought would hurt her. I pretty well did as much as I could to keep up with the job description of the mother of the century. I was young, idealistic, and had the energy. At the time, I had no exposure to any alternative ideologies on how to mother, so I was swept up with the societal messages of the perfect mother.

My first act of resistance against society's expectations on me as a mother occurred when I was pregnant with my second daughter,

Leigh-Ann. One morning, Stephanie asked me if she could be present at the birth of her sister. After doing some research and exploring whether it would be safe for Stephanie, my partner and I decided to go ahead with a sibling-witnessed birth. I was questioned by many who believed I was crazy to include Stephanie in the birth of her sister. They said I would damage her and that I was being irresponsible. For the first time I began to catch on to the rigidity of the rules and expectations that society had placed on me as a mother. But because I felt convinced that allowing Stephanie to be part of her sister's birth was a good idea, I stood my ground. Stephanie was one of the first people to ever touch her sister; she was there to caress Leigh-Ann's sticky body seconds after she came into the world. This by far is one of the most memorable moments of my life. This first act of resistance against societal expectations felt good and empowering although I had a long way to go before I became fully aware that I was practicing a very sacrificial style of mothering.

At age 27, I had two amazing girls and a comfortable life in the suburbs of Vancouver, British Columbia. Three weeks before Leigh-Ann was born, I graduated with my Bachelor of Arts in Psychology. I wanted to be home with my girls, but given how demanding the job of mothering was, I couldn't tolerate being home all the time. This choice foreshadowed my eventual decision to resist societal expectations to stay home full-time when my children were young. I decided to find a learning opportunity that was related to my goal of becoming a counsellor. When Leigh-Ann was only a few months old, I enrolled in several process-oriented counselling courses. This meant that the students participated in therapy concurrently with their counselling training. After a few classes, I noticed that much of the sorrow the participants shared in therapy was related to their childhoods, to things they claimed their parents had done or not done for them. The pain and distress over how they had been parented led to my own concern that my daughters would one day grow up to feel that way about me. Could I parent my girls so that they would never need therapy? Now there was a thought! If I understood how people were traumatized and what nurtures them and applied this knowledge within my own family, my children would never need to go to therapy! I often tell this story to the parent groups I lead and they almost always break into roaring laughter. But I doubt that I was alone in my expectations.

Many parents who had their children in the 1980s heard or read about the "wounded inner child" that John Bradshaw so passionately spoke about in his PBS television series and books (Bradshaw, 1992). Suggesting that all the ills of society were due to poor mothering or dysfunctional parenting, he solidified the idea that mothers are damaging and at fault for all addictions and depressions. It made mothers fear that they would damage their children. The idea that parents create "wounded" children seeped into our consciousness. My exposure to John Bradshaw's work certainly impacted me. I did not want to wound my children. I believed I could prevent this if only I could be the perfect mother.

Clearly, I was blind to how narrow and destructive this perspective was. Not only did I apply every piece of "psychological expert knowledge" I got my hands on, I decided that I would dedicate my career to helping parents raise children who would never need therapy. I developed a ten-week parent education course based on attachment theory, developmental psychology, and parental self-awareness and personal growth.

Attachment, according to John Bowlby (1991), is central to human development. The theory suggests that healthy, responsible parents develop secure attachments with their children. A secure attachment, according to the theory, is the foundation of development because it allows children to feel safe in the world. The theory assures us that securely attached children are able to engage in developmental tasks with confidence, which leads to a sense of competence and high self worth. Although no one debates the value of love and attachment in the lives of children, over the last 30 years this theory has complicated things for mothers because many of us end up sacrificing our own well-being in the name of "loving" our children. In my early years as a mother, I became convinced that love and sacrifice, if necessary, would conquer all. I became overly vigilant about my "attachment" with my daughters and emphasized the importance of secure attachment to the parents who attended my parenting courses.

In my late 20s, my awareness of how little mothers are valued grew when I examined the literature on parental experience. I wanted to include some information on parental experience in my parent education course, so I read extensively on the topic. What was interesting at the time, and still holds today, is that the popular and academic literature on parenting and families focused on children, and very little on the experiences of mothers, their needs, what allowed them to parent well, and what made parenting difficult. In other words, it was all about the children, whereas the parents' experience, their needs, the impact of their personalities, history, and current life stressors were ignored. It was then that I began to realize that mothers were oppressed and excluded from the public sphere (Douglas and Michaels, 2004). I began to see that mothers were so occupied trying to meet all the requirements of the job that they had no energy left to care for themselves, participate in society, or nurture their adult relationships. This insight was a key factor in my evolving interest in the experience of mothers, and eventually becoming an advocate for their well-being.

For the past 20 years, I have been offering parenting courses, workshops, and talks on the topic of parenting and mothering. The content and focus has shifted from teaching mothers how to apply developmental psychology to raising children while also developing self-awareness, to researching and speaking against the societal oppression to which mothers are subjected. What has been unique about my work as a parent educator is that I have added mothers and their personal histories, personalities, and stresses to the equation of parenting. I have also encouraged them to explore societal and historical factors that affect mothering practices in order to question what is expected of them. This is a departure from most of the information directed at mothers, which focuses on children and their needs. Although my initial interest was to teach mothers how to be "good" mothers, I eventually caught on to the oppression associated with all the messages directed at mothers. When I developed this awareness, I shifted my focus to helping mothers free themselves from this oppression. As for my dream to raise my daughters without ever needing to go to therapy, I have since abandoned that goal, but I joke about it with my girls all the time. I once said to Leigh-Ann, "When you are sitting in that therapist's office, telling her how angry you are at me, just remember this moment when I am sticking spots on this Dalmatian Halloween costume!"

I have come a long way from the days when I endeavoured to be the mother of the century. My education and research were instrumental in my growth. For example, both of my graduate theses were on mothering. My Master's thesis investigated the experience of mothers in stepfamilies, and my Ph.D. dissertation, which is the basis for this book, addressed the experience of mothers who questioned and resisted the current dominant discourse of motherhood (I will define this shortly). Ironically, the idea for my Ph.D. research came to me during one of those days when I was striving to be the "mother of the century." I followed my daughters from store to store, being patient, struggling to know when to get excited about a piece of clothing they were trying on and when to be honest if it didn't look good. As we were walking, we passed a bookstore that had a clearance sale. I rarely have the patience to look in the bins full of books that are in no particular order. But that day, it gave me a break from following the girls around, at least for a few minutes. As if placed there by the hand of God, I found a book, *The Myths of Motherhood: How Culture Reinvents the Good Mother* by Shari Thurer (1994). I immediately bought it, and savoured the thought of sitting in peace and reading about the history of motherhood.

Reading Shari Thurer's (1994) book helped me realize that there was such a thing as a set of myths that had evolved into a powerful dominant discourse of motherhood. Thurer referred to this phenomenon as the "myths of motherhood," which has also been referred to as the institution of motherhood (Rich, 1986), the ideology of intensive mothering (Hays, 1996), patriarchal motherhood (O'Reilly, 2004, 2010), the new momism (Douglas and Michaels, 2004), and the dominant discourse of motherhood (Horwitz, 2003). All of these terms refer to a set of tenets that are meant to convince mothers that practicing intensive mothering (Hays) is the one and only right way to mother. This parenting model, as Hays suggests, is intensive and child-centred. Within this model, mothers ignore their own needs and spend most of their time, energy, and financial resources on their children. Intensive mothering is laborious, expert guided, and emotionally taxing (Hays, 1996). It expects mothers to be ever-present, empathic, patient, sacrificial, selfless, devoted solely to their children, and role models.

I learned that mothering is surely a maze, full of complicated questions and demands. I began to understand that mothers are constantly faced with making decisions for which there are no guaranteed outcomes. They expend significant energy sorting through the many expectations set for them. When engaged in the job of mothering, mothers try to find their way inside the maze of possibilities that impact them and their children. I began to see that the problem was that mothers were pressured by an ideal that expects them to be perfect therapists, pediatricians, and teachers, and to devote all of their physical, emotional, and financial energy to their children (Douglas and Michaels, 2004; Hays, 1996). I was able to appreciate that on one hand, this ideal mesmerizes mothers into believing that if they meet all these expectations they will raise super children. On the other hand, society blames them when things go "wrong" with their kids. I realized that the combination of these two opposing possibilities made it impossible for mothers to "win" and feel at peace.

Thurer's book changed my life personally, academically, and professionally. It inspired me so much that, not only did I begin to consciously resist the dominant discourse, I also decided that through my research I would learn how to empower mothers. As I read the book, I became aware that women have mothered very differently throughout history. I began to realize that my belief that there was one right way to mother was false. Not only that, but I also realized that mothering practices throughout history have been influenced by social, political, and economic factors, which means that we really don't have an answer to the question: what is the best way to mother?

A cursive exploration of how mothers have cared for their children over the centuries or across cultures reveals that the expectations set out by the modern institution of motherhood are culturally and politically constructed and not the sole, right way to mother children. There have always been physical, social, economic, and cultural factors that have impacted mothers and their maternal practices. In the next few paragraphs, I briefly outline examples of maternal practices and views of family and children in order to illustrate that there have been many different ways to mother. This is not intended to be a full historical account or portrait of motherhood but rather a cursory exploration of some examples of mothering practices. My purpose is to illustrate that maternal practices are diverse, an awareness that can be freeing (Porter, 2010) by creating possibilities for mothers to explore alternatives to the current dominant discourse of motherhood.

Family configurations and the role of children in families have varied significantly throughout history. For example, in the West, since the Medieval Period (sixth century) and until the Industrial Revolution (late eighteenth century, early nineteenth century), the family worked together and consisted of several children and a few adults within a community (Badinter, 1981; Thurer, 1994). Families during these centuries were large and consisted of several generations. Their homes were not exclusive to the nuclear family and were not divided into private rooms; most members ate and slept in the same room. Families during this period continued to be economically connected and worked together in the fields, the home, and every other endeavour necessary to keep the family and community safe. Given the economic need for "hands," families had many children because of the fact that only a few survived. Furthermore, marriage was mainly an arrangement based on material needs. Life expectancy during those times was short and many adults died young, which meant that there were few adults to take care of all the children. This meant that children did not receive the type or amount of attention they receive today and mothers could not invest a lot of time or effort in their children (Badinter, 1981; Hays, 1996; Thurer, 1994).

After the Industrial Revolution (nineteenth century) when fathers began to leave the home to work in factories, the communal family and the expectations on mothers changed (Thurer, 1994). The family no longer worked together to produce the goods needed to feed and care for its members. Instead, families moved to urban centres where fathers were employed in factories, leaving mothers to run the home. Families were now expected to be consumers of goods rather than producers of their own. This meant that families had to earn money so fathers became the main breadwinners and mothers were relegated as homemakers (O'Reilly, 2004). By moving to urban centres, families became separate private entities losing the community they had in more rural settings. As the family changed, their energy shifted from focusing on the production of goods to other functions.

The socialization of children became a central importance at this time because the structure of families was transformed by the Industrial Revolution (Hays, 1996; O'Reilly, 2004; Thurer, 1994). Fathers lost some of their authority by being largely absent, in contrast with the father of colonial times (sixteenth and seventeenth centuries) who was involved in rocking his babies to sleep and in charge of instilling moral values on the children (Eyer, 1996). It was also at this time that children began to be seen as precious and innocent, in need of being protected, and with their childhood respected as a unique stage. Middle class mothers were now expected to be home to care for their children. Mothers for the first time found themselves forced to fulfill all the newly defined "needs" of their children by themselves. But although mothers were home, they were largely occupied with housework and the maintenance of their home; they were not devoting all their time to attending to or spending time with their children. Rather, they expected children to participate in the many chores needed to run the home. This was the beginning of the modern mother as we know her today.

The idea of the "stay-at-home" mother has historically only been accessible to wealthy or upper middle class women. For most of history, mothers who did not belong to the wealthy, bourgeois classes were unable to stay home and meet the expectation of being the sole nurturer of children (Thurer, 1994). They had to earn money along with their husbands by working jobs that were low-paying and exploitative.

In the West, even the white, middle-class mothers of the 1950s mothered differently from the contemporary middle class mother. They were expected to keep the house clean, cook good meals, and look attractive for their husbands when they returned home from work (White, 1950). *The Globe and Mail* published an article on December 11, 1950 (p.16) that spoke about the "modern woman" who had "to work harder to keep her marriage intact" by keeping up with "her husband's business and social life," by being attractive at all times "as walking proof that he is a good provider" (White, 1950). Adele White emphasized the importance of the "modern woman" staying home with her children in order to avoid divorce and maintain a solid marriage. Women in the 1950s were exposed to these types of messages and expectations, but they were in no way expected to mother intensely by stimulating their children constantly, spending quality time, being emotionally available, spending copious amounts of money on gadgets for their kids, or taking them to a variety of after-school activities. These mothers were expected to be good at domesticity (i.e., cooking, cleaning) and catering to their husbands.

It is apparent that economic, political, technological, and social factors have impacted the family structure and societal expectations on mothers throughout history. These factors tend to lead to many different consequences for women whose mothering practices vary depending on what is happening socially, economically, and politically in their world. Given all these factors and the diversity of mothering practices throughout history, it is difficult to identify one right way to mother. In fact *all* cultures, each with their distinct political, economic, and structural contexts, tend to develop rules of conduct for mothers. In most cases, each promotes its own rules as the right way to mother.

But I argue that there is no one right way to mother, evidenced by a few examples of differing maternal practices in history and various cultures. Mothering practices across cultures, for example, range from communal mothering in Africa (Bernard, 1974; Mawami, 2001) to the exclusive, intensive mothering in North America (Chase and Rogers, 2001; Hays, 1996; Rich, 1986; Walls, 2010). Mothers in different cultures care for their children in very different ways. Mothers are influenced by their culture, environmental context, economic position, class, religious beliefs, political climate, and so on. For example, the Nyansongo mothers of Kenya work in the fields and around their home while child nurses carry and care for their infant children (Bernard, 1974). This child nurse is usually the infant's sibling who is between six and ten years old and plays an important part in the infant's life. Mothers in these communities are usually burdened with intense agricultural work and they therefore reduce their maternal role to its bare essentials.

Another example is from Japan where the care of children in the village of Taira, Okinawa is shared between parents, paternal grandparents, aunts, and uncles (Bernard, 1974). Children expect guidance and discipline from all these different family members rather than just from their parents. Their experience of growing up within a philosophy of collectivity leads to a collective identity rather than an individualistic one. These children's behaviour is molded by their sense of duty towards their family and not by their desire to meet their needs before the needs of their community.

One additional instance of more communal parenting is that of the Tarong in the Philippines who do not allow mothers to have sole responsibility for their children. To these people, making mothers solely responsible for the upbringing of their children would be unthinkable. Fathers, siblings, aunts, and grandmothers are involved in caretaking (Bernard, 1974). One need not go too far to find cultural or ideological groups who practice mothering in ways that depart from the Western dominant ideology.

In North America, for example, many African American women hold values and beliefs that are different from the Western dominant discourse of motherhood. African American mothers are often viewed as a source of growth, hope, status, and power in their community (Thomas, 2000). Many African American mothers believe that the Black community should work together to raise their children and that motherhood should not be the exclusive responsibility of one mother (Edwards, 2000; Thomas, 2000). Many mothers within this group practice what Edwards calls "othermothering." In an article she published in the *Journal for the Association for Research on Mothering*, Edwards defines othermothering as involving the provision of the care of children by extended family and other non-blood friends or neighbors. Moreover, Edwards explains that the view that motherhood is "one's true and only occupation is a view that few African American women have wanted to adopt" (p.59). Many African American women value self-sufficiency, independence, and personal accomplishment, as well as nurturing and caring. Even though they have been exposed to the ideal of self-sacrifice, many African American women do not embrace this view. For many of them, guilty feelings are absent when, for example, they leave their children to go to work. Additionally, employment is a way of life, not a choice that can harm their children. In sum, many African American mothers appear to have found ways to mother that are influenced by their history and societal conditions and that challenge the current expectations on mothers to be the sole caretakers, the best and only nurturers of children, and to be ever-present.

One can also find diverse mothering practices and beliefs in Canadian society. For example, many mothers from various cultures draw from their religious and cultural beliefs to guide their mothering. Farah Mawami (2001) conducted a research project in Canada titled *Sharing Attachment Practices across Cultures: Learning from Immigrants and Refugees*. She reports that Muslim parents from various countries who now live in Canada, for example, follow their religion's dictates when it comes to the values they transmit to their children, or how they interact with them. Some mothers from India and other Asian countries sometimes leave their children behind in their countries when they immigrate to Canada. Even though these mothers report that they love their children, leaving them behind to be cared for by other family members is necessary for them. They feel their children will eventually benefit when mother and child are reunited in Canada. Many immigrants to Canada also believe that childcare is the responsibility of the community. Mawami quotes a mother saying:

> In my home country, neighbours took our children for a while. There were more people to shower love on a child. Here there is only the father and mother. And they are too busy. There are only the parents to show bonding to a child. (p. 35)

Other immigrants believe that extended families can be helpful in mediating relationships between mothers and children. In other words, they welcome the input and interventions of others after giving birth and throughout the development of their children. They do not believe in the exclusivity of mothering.

These are only a few examples of the diversity in mothering practices across the globe. What this diversity indicates is that there are many different ways in which children are raised and that various environmental, social, cultural, and familial demands influence these practices. In other words, different mothering practices will take shape based on when and where they happen. The beliefs about mothering and the practices that accompany them are highly influenced by society, the historical period in which they occur, and the culture that promotes them, not to mention patriarchal forces. This diversity of mothering practices throughout history and in different cultures suggests that there isn't one right way to mother. Furthermore, this shows that there are multiple options available, so that one can assume that even though a society expects us to mother by the tenets of an ideal, we can engage in alternative ways of mothering that may be more satisfying for both mothers and their children. One of these options is resistance, which can help mothers reduce the oppressive power of the current dominant discourse of motherhood.

This book is about resistance to the dominant discourse of motherhood. About how resistance works, how it is experienced, and what supports mothers in their struggle to resist. When I began the study, little was known about the process of resistance, the factors at play, and how people who resist see themselves. My research examines how some mothers who were in the process of resistance discovered that their resistance empowered them.

What do I mean by resistance? Many of the publications that offer a critique of the institution of motherhood portray mothers as passive victims who may have no recourse against such a powerful force. However, human beings have historically resisted societal oppression (Foucault, 1984) and mothers are no exception (Gordon, 1990; Green, 2009; Horwitz, 2003; Horwitz and Long, 2005). Resistance in this context is the effort of oppressed groups to challenge and act against aspects of the dominant discourse (Scott, 1990). In other words, resistance is the conscious choice to challenge and act against social expectations by questioning the status quo and choosing alternative actions. This book describes how some women experienced their resistance against the dominant discourse of motherhood. The women I interviewed identified themselves as consciously resisting some aspects of this societal ideal of motherhood and the myths that are contained within it. In other words, these women had caught on to many of the social expectations and were making conscious choices to challenge some of them.

While the dominant discourse of motherhood is also known as the ideology of intensive mothering, the institution of motherhood, patriarchal motherhood and the new momism, for the remainder of the book, I will use the term *dominant discourse of motherhood*. Discourse can be defined as a specific set of statements, terms, and categories that are specific to a historical period and a particular society (Foucault, 1984; Scott, 1990). Discourses are messages and societal beliefs that create rules and expectations of behavior and ways of thinking. Like stories, they create common understandings of who holds societal power within relationships and of appropriate rules of conduct (Robinson and Robinson, 1998). The dominant discourse of motherhood, therefore, sets rules and expectations about how a mother should behave, how she should think about being a mother, and the nature of her relationship with her children. It projects the understanding that mothers must focus on the private world of home and their children and relinquish their social power in the name of caring for their children.

A close examination of social discourses reveals that there are a multitude of them. For example, there are the discourses of childhood, success, femininity, masculinity, love, the working woman, and so on. Some discourses tend to be more dominant and central while others are more marginal or alternative (Foucault, 1984; Little, 1999). For instance, the dominant discourse of motherhood is the most widely accepted and promoted in our Western society, whereas a discourse of queer motherhood is more marginal. It is because of this array of discourses that people are able to note contradictions and gaps within dominant discourses, which then allows them to challenge their oppressive tenets. In many cases, people are able to resist society's dominant discourses by drawing on other alternative discourses. It is in this manner that people are agents in their own lives rather than passive victims of these discourses. For example, feminists have engaged in agentic activity by drawing on discourses of equality and human rights to challenge aspects of the dominant patriarchal discourse. They have critiqued motherhood as an oppressive institution that limits mothers to the private sphere and keeps them from influencing public processes or policies that affect their lives (Rich, 1986).

The women who I interviewed engaged in agented action by drawing on several other discourses to resist and develop their own constructions of maternal philosophy and practice. This act of resistance led all of them to feel empowered. I must note that agency in this sense is constrained by the discourses that are available to us at the time. In other words, agency exists within the current societal discourses one can draw from. One of the most significant findings (which I will discuss in more detail later in the book) is that all the women who participated in the study felt empowered by the act of resistance. How they resisted, how effective their resistance was, or how difficult it was to resist did not have an impact on their experience of empowerment. They felt empowered because they felt they were actively questioning societal expectations and the act of questioning and making their own choices felt significantly empowering to them.

This finding is consistent with a larger conversation about empowered mothering and feminist mothering among scholars and feminists. Adrienne Rich was the first to make the distinction between the institution of motherhood that is oppressive to mothers and the loving and nurturing act of caring for children (1986). The former is dictated by a patriarchal, male agenda whereas the latter, the act of mothering, is defined by the experience of mothering itself and the love for our children. Rich was also the first to suggest that mothering can be a site of empowerment for women whereas the institution is disempowering and oppressive (1986; O'Reilly, 2004). Andrea O'Reilly, President of the Motherhood Initiative for Research and Community Involvement (MIRCI, formerly the Association for Research on Mothering or ARM), has also contributed greatly to this conversation by grappling with the distinction and similarities of empowered mothering and feminist mothering. She opens the introduction to her book, *Mother Outlaws*, by explaining that the modern ideal of intensive mothering is not about the nurturing and loving aspect of mothering but about the oppressive and disempowering patriarchal institution of motherhood (O'Reilly, 2004). She suggests that empowered mothers will endeavour to deconstruct and eliminate patriarchal motherhood to open the way for new, more empowered narratives of mothering. In this sense, both feminist and resistant mothers are empowered mothers. It follows then, that all feminist mothers are empowered mothers but not all empowered mothers are feminist mothers.

I define empowerment as a woman's ability to influence her life and make choices that are in line with her needs, vision, values, and rights. In other words, empowerment is about having and using the tools necessary to influence one's life in a desired direction. Feminist mothering is defined as maternal practice that not only resists the dominant discourse of motherhood, but also raises children in a way that teaches them a feminist analysis of privilege and power (Green, 2009). Feminist mothers are empowered mothers, but not all empowered mothers may be feminist mothers: some of the women who I interviewed identified as feminist and some did not. The original purpose of the study was to investigate the experience of mothers who were resisting the dominant discourse and did not seek to investigate the experience of feminist mothers.

In sum, in this book I examine the experience of resisting the dominant discourse of motherhood, the diverse practices of resistance in which these women engaged, and the personal, contextual, and situational factors that supported their resistance. A key overarching finding is that all these mothers felt empowered as a result of their resistance because they were active in the process of mothering rather than passive victims of the expectations placed upon them by society.

This book is about giving voice to a group of mothers who caught on to how society tries to control their mothering practices and decided to resist that control. It is about the possibility that the average mother (not only the educated, feminist, activist, white, middle-class mother) can question a dominant discourse and take part in resistance to it. By writing this book, I hope to contribute to the average mother's life and also to the growing discussion on the empowerment of mothers, and for the growth and betterment of women in general. The analysis of the interviews yielded significant information about the process of resistance, its complexities, and the gifts and the challenges of resistance. Furthermore, it opened a window to the understanding that resistance is not a process that occurs completely outside of the dominant discourse; all the women I interviewed resisted aspects of the discourse but also complied with some of its tenets. The study revealed that resistance is not all rosy, but rather comes with its own challenges and difficulties.

I hope that this book lands in the hands of many mothers so as to advance our conversations about mothering and empowerment. I don't expect to promote one new way to mother. I hope that all mothers will critique those societal expectations that are aimed at controlling their mothering practices. The dominant discourse of which I speak in this book is the white, middle-class, and Western model of motherhood. It aims to influence all mothers in the West regardless of their background. It is the dominant model against which most maternal practices are evaluated. So whether a mother is practicing mothering from this perspective or not, I hope that this book opens, inspires or initiates conversations at the playground, gatherings, or work. If we talk about mothering and open ourselves to the possibility that mothering can be practiced in many different ways, we may indeed change the course of the discourse.

In Chapter 1, I focus on the dominant discourse of motherhood. I provide an account of how this discourse evolved over the past 30 years and of the social, economic, and political forces that influenced its evolution. I discuss the current definitions of "mother" and present statistics that indicate that women today are still doing most of the caregiving for children and their homes even in two-parent families. In addition, I argue that the current reality of mothers in trying to achieve the ideal of the perfect mother limits their potential and leads to significant stress and guilt.

In Chapter 2, I present the experience of mothering under the pressure of the dominant discourse of motherhood. I discuss literature and research studies that indicate that mothers who aspire to live by the ideal of this discourse tend to experience guilt, depression, fatigue, and anguish.

In Chapter 3, I describe how some mothers have deviated from the dominant discourse of motherhood and engaged in a process of resistance. I present different examples of *how* they resisted. These mothers questioned the status quo and took risks by making decisions that were not within society's expectations on how mothers should parent.

In Chapter 4, I describe what the experience of resistance was like for these women, including a range of consequences of resistance, many positive and some more challenging. This chapter conveys that resisting dominant ideologies in society can be very empowering and liberating and yet difficult at times. I provide many examples of how the women in the study handled these issues.

Chapter 5 is based on the premise that in order to resist, mothers must draw on various discourses available to them. In this chapter, I illuminate several discourses that influenced these mothers. Because people have access to a range of discourses to help them construct their realities, it is useful to explore what discourses influenced these mothers, the types of identities they had developed, and how they wove their own fabric of parenting by drawing from both the dominant discourse and others. I also discuss instances of compliance to the dominant discourse and highlight that none of them existed fully outside of this discourse.

Chapter 6 presents the factors that facilitated these mothers' resistance. In order to resist, I found that these mothers relied on a series of situational, structural, and personal factors. Factors such as partners, spouses, family support, education, and early life experiences are discussed.

Finally in Chapter 7, I summarize and address some key points so as to provide some insights about what the findings of my study may mean for mothers, social change, and those interested in advancing our understanding of mothers' resistance through their research and social activism endeavours.

My hope in writing this book is that it will encourage the empowerment of mothers and contribute to the larger conversation about mothers' realities. Moreover, I hope to encourage a process of resistance against the dominant discourse of motherhood that causes so much pressure and anxiety. By questioning this discourse and making conscious decisions as to how they want to mother, women can be empowered to make a difference in their own lives and in society as a whole. I want mothers to unite in support of one another rather than sit in judgment and criticism. My study suggests that when women question the status quo and make their own choices they feel empowered and confident about how they are mothering, which appears to help them deal with pressures society places on them. I hope you join me in this journey of discovery, self-reflection, and hope.

Chapter 1

The Dominant Discourse of Motherhood

We all know the ideal of the good mother. Above all, she is selfless. Her children come before herself and any other need or person or commitment, no matter what. She loves her children unconditionally yet she is careful not to smother them with love and her own needs. She follows the advice of doctors and other experts and she educates herself about child development. She is ever-present in her children's lives when they are young, and when they get older she is home every day to greet them as they return from school. If she works outside the home, she arranges her job around her children so she can be there for them as much as possible, certainly whenever they are sick or unhappy. The good mother's success is reflected in her children's behavior—they are well mannered and respectful to others; at the same time they have a strong sense of independence and self esteem. They grow up to be productive citizens. (Chase and Rogers, 2001, p. 30)

NEED I SAY MORE? WE ALL want to be *good* mothers, don't we? We want to raise children who are healthy, able to take care of themselves, happy, with high self-esteem, well educated, successful, and so on. Mothers today assume that wanting these things is an intrinsic part of being a mother (Thurer, 1994). While many believe that mothers have always felt this way about their children and about being mothers (Bowlby, 1991; Sears and Sears, 2001), this is simply not the case. As we have seen, mothers have mothered differently throughout history and in different cultures, and today is no exception.

Mothers in the Western world are influenced by a discourse emphasizing sacrifice and perfection, and which is laden with a series of myths. We call them myths because, although they are believed to be true, they often are not. In other words, myths are false collective beliefs that are used to justify a social ideology. Within the dominant discourse of motherhood, myths set up a premise that a mother must give up her selfhood; she must give up her agency, authority, autonomy, and authenticity (O'Reilly, 2004). Given this fact, questioning the dominant discourse of motherhood and these myths might free mothers to make conscious choices about how they want to practice mothering. In this chapter, I examine the dominant discourse of motherhood, which also interacts and is supported by other dominant discourses such as the discourse of the successful woman, the discourse of childhood, the discourse of the happy family, and the discourse of independence among others. I discuss and incorporate these in Chapter 5. The next section provides a brief summary of the tenets contained in the dominant discourse of motherhood.

A Description of the Dominant Discourse of Motherhood

The Western, white, middle-class dominant discourse of motherhood is made up of a series of tenets that are aimed at mothers. These tenets are rules of conduct and maternal practice that mothers are expected to follow. These tenets include: mothers are fully responsible; mothers should be empathic; mothers should be ever-present; mothers should put their children's needs first; mothers are to blame for anything that goes wrong with their children; mothers should consult expert advice; mothers should provide strong attachments; mothers should be careful not to over attach; mothers should be home as much as possible; mothers should avoid raising the "wounded inner child;" mothers should make sure they provide enough stimulation; mothers should recognize that children are fragile; and mothers should be good mothers and good workers (Horwitz, 2003). I now provide a brief description of each of these.

Fully responsible

The myths of motherhood suggest that mothers are responsible for the physical, spiritual, and psychological well being of their children (Douglas and Michaels, 2004; Gleason, 1999; Hays, 1996; Thurer, 1994). Mothers today take this responsibility very seriously. They worry about providing 'quality' time, nutrition, stimulation (e.g., read, buy educational, fun toys, videos, go to the park, bake with them, and so on), empathy, good communication, designer clothing, and more (Douglas and Michaels, 2004; Thurer, 1994). What is more, this idea that they are fully responsible puts mothers at the receiving end of blame when anything goes wrong with their children.

Empathy

There are many mothering practices related to caring for a child's psychological well being that are driven by the discourse. At first glance these appear to be common sense and certainly conducive to good outcomes. One such example is the communication of empathy and understanding toward our children. Empathy refers to putting oneself in the other person's shoes, imagining what they are feeling, and then conveying this back to them (Greenberg, 1996). Mothers today are told that they need to be empathic toward their children. This, it is said, is part of their responsibility toward their children's psychological well-being. By being empathic, mothers teach their children about feelings, about feeling understood and cared for. And yet, the expectation of being an empathic mother has led mothers to pressure themselves to always be "on" and never "lose it" on their children. What is more, when a mother is unable to be empathic she feels tremendous guilt (Eyer, 1996; Seagram and Daniluk, 2002).

Mothers need to be ever-present and do it all

The dominant discourse of motherhood promotes the expectation that mothers are required to be ever-present, sacrificial, and all loving (Contratto, 1984). It emphasizes the idea that mothers should be the central caregivers of their children because "mothers know best" (Ranson, 1999). Mothers believe that they are the best sources of love, guidance and nurturing for their children because they gave birth to them (Thurer, 1994). The belief that it is exclusively a mother's love that can prevent all problems and meet all of a child's needs is a tall order. Many women who have attended my speaking engagements tell me they are always the ones taking care of most of their children needs: reading to them, hugging them, bathing them, finding them daycare, talking to the teachers, going to school functions, empathizing with them when they are upset, making doctor's appointments, taking them to appointments, teaching them to cooperate at home, making sure they do their homework, booking babysitters, making lunches and dinners, grocery shopping, cleaning their homes, and so on. In many cases, husbands participate in some tasks but not enough. According to Canadian statistics, mothers are still doing much more than their partners when it comes to child-care and house-hold work. In Canada, women who are employed outside of the home work an equivalent of 1,314 hours per year more than their husbands in child and home related work (Marshall, 2006). So it is still a reality that women continue to work long hours in home and child care even when they are employed full-time. This second-shift means that most employed women come home from work, change *hats,* and work some more as mothers and housekeepers (Hochschild and Machung, 2003). All this in the name of duty. A duty that is dictated by the myth that mothers are the best caregivers of children and responsible for their physical, psychological, and emotional well-being.

A child's needs always come first

Now, the problem isn't only that mothers are expected to do all this but also that they are expected to do it even if it means they will stop attending to their own needs (Contratto, 1984; Douglas and Michaels, 2004; Hays, 1996; O'Reilly, 2004). In other words, a woman's needs stop counting once she has children; mothers are so blinded by the dominant discourse of motherhood that they rarely attempt to make their needs count. Society does not take mothers' contributions as valuable or worthwhile. And to make matters worse, a mother who "fails" to take care of her children's needs to perfection is regarded by others as selfish and uncaring (Gleason, 1999; Maushart, 2000).

Blame

One of the most devastating tenets of the dominant discourse is the idea that mothers are at fault for any psychological or behavioural difficulties in their children (Contratto, 1984; Thurer, 1994). The power of the discourse has led mothers to aspire to be "perfect mothers." They make every effort to avoid making mistakes while raising their children because any mistake can lead to behavioural, mood, relational, and many other types of psychological problems (Contratto, 1984; Croghan and Miell, 1998; Thurer, 1994). This myth suggests that mothers are powerful forces that can harm their children (Coontz, 1992; Weingarten, 1995). So mothers worry not only about doing the right thing, but also about NOT doing the wrong thing. Many believe that any mistake can affect their children's self-esteem, their confidence, their ability to form healthy relationships, or can lead to depression, and other psychological disorders (Contratto, 1984; Thurer, 1994). Mothers today are perceived not only as the primary driving force in their children's development but also as the primary obstacle.

Mothers must consult expert advice

There are other messages implied in this "mother as powerful agent" idea. Because mothers are viewed as overly responsible for the fate of their children, they are told they must *learn* how to parent (Arnup, 1994; Hays, 1996; O'Reilly, 2004). In order to satisfy this expectation, mothers are supposed to turn to an endless list of experts such as psychologists, physicians, and educators (Arnup, 1994; Hays, 1996; Thurer, 1994). They are expected to seek advice in countless books, manuals, and parenting courses. The information in childcare manuals, for example, is often conflicting and overwhelming but always carries one overall message: It is up to mothers to nurture, love, care for, and stimulate their children, or the children will be greatly damaged (Contratto, 1984; Douglas and Michaels, 2004; Eyer, 1996; Hays, 1996; Thurer, 1994). This vast amount of mothering advice has left mothers feeling inadequate and unable to trust their instincts given they could harm their children if they do not consult these "experts" (Arnup, 1994). The impossibility of living up to the ideal set forth by expert advice places mothers in a constant state of self-doubt.

In her book, *Perfect Madness*, Judith Warner (2006) described the degree of anxiety and stress that mothers today are experiencing mostly due to their attempts to meet the standards set by much of the "expert" advice on how they should mother and the larger discourse of motherhood.

A mother must develop strong attachments with her children

The expectation that we will love our children unconditionally and sacrificially was promoted by John Bowlby's attachment theory (Bowlby, 1991). Expert advice, based on Bowlby's theory of attachment, informs mothers that bonding with their children is essential. Mothers are told that spending copious amounts of time developing this bond is very important because when it fails to form, children are at risk of developing serious psychological problems (Bowlby, 1991). Mothers today endeavour to dedicate time and energy to the formation of this bond and often wonder if they have covered all the basics. Many mothers anxiously evaluate on a daily basis whether they are parenting adequately or whether their children are developing successfully (Contratto, 1984; Warner, 2006).

Attach, but not too much

At the same time that mothers are expected to create these strong, secure attachments, they are also expected to encourage independence. They are to avoid over-nurturing because this can lead to immaturity and dependence in their children (Chase and Rogers, 2001). So a child who is "immature" or dependent is seen as having been "spoiled" and too pampered (Chase and Rogers, 2001).

You should be at home with the children as much as possible

In addition to having to love our children unconditionally, the ideas behind attachment theory have led some mothers to worry about not being with their children all the time. Mothers are made to feel guilty when they choose not to be or are unable to be the main presence in their children's lives. Many mothers who work outside of the home have to deal with the ongoing guilt of leaving their children in the care of others (Bernard, 1974; Coontz, 1992; Hays, 1996; McMahon, 1995; Seagram and Daniluk, 2002).

If you don't do it right, you may raise a "wounded" child

The idea that childhood problems may create a wounded inner child further compounds the pressures on mothers (Coontz, 1992). During the 1980s and '90s, John Bradshaw (1992) claimed that the reason why adults experience depression, addictions, and other problems is because they have a wounded inner child who was hurt and damaged by their parents. Bradshaw asserted that the major source of human suffering is this "neglected, wounded child." Given this philosophy, today's mothers have been told that their own mothers are to blame for their psychological distress, their problems with relationships, etc. This blaming, in turn, places the present generation of mothers as the potentially blamed mothers of the future. The fear of making mistakes or not doing the right thing for their children has lead mothers not only to feel guilty but to worry about their every move (Warner, 2006). This fear of being the bad, blamed mother has pushed mothers to overindulge their children, to struggle to set boundaries, to be overly empathic, and to live with a high level of anxiety (Warner, 2006).

Mothers must provide the right amount of stimulation for their children

Mothers have also been told that stimulating their infants to enhance their development and learning is essential to healthy development (Thurer, 1994). Experts tell mothers to talk to their babies, play with them, and encourage their intellectual growth so they grow into intelligent adults (Arnup, 1994). As a result, mothers are left wondering how much "stimulation" is enough.

Children are fragile

In addition to the dominant discourse of motherhood, mothers are simultaneously influenced by other discourses that interact with it. For example, related to the dominant discourse of motherhood are the ideas on childhood and children's needs (Badinter, 1981; Contratto, 1994; Coontz, 1992; Fass and Mason, 2000; Hays, 1996). They are regarded as beings who deserve to be protected from all harm and indulged to enjoy their childhood. Adults are told that they must handle all children with patience regardless of their behaviour because children need to be properly guided by positive models (Arnup, 1994). If a mother raises her voice or is not able to keep her composure she is made to feel guilty because "losing it" can be damaging to her children (Coontz, 1992, p. 225).

Mothers who work should be good mothers and good workers

To complicate matters, given the necessity for many women to work for pay, the contradictions between the discourses of the working/professional woman and motherhood exacerbate their ability to mother without guilt and stress. The expectations on mothers who work outside of the home are often contradictory to the expectations on mothers in general (Baber and Allen, 1992; Douglas and Michaels, 2004; Hays, 1996; Maushart, 2000). Many mothers who work outside of the home are torn between their obligations at work and at home. At the same time, some mothers who stay home often feel deficient because they do not pursue a career (Hays, 1996). Furthermore, as Sharon Hays suggests in her book, *The Cultural Contradictions of Motherhood*, the philosophy of the workplace is based on a self-interested, profit-maximizing utility. Many mothers are led to believe they must perform to their maximum potential in the workplace. In addition, they must act quite differently in each role, competitive and tough-minded at work, and warm and loving at home (Douglas and Michaels, 2004; Hays, 1996). In trying to integrate both their mothering and working roles, mothers often feel that their children should always come first. However, they often feel that they are not fulfilling either role to the best of their ability, often falling short of the expectations (Hays, 1996). The contradictions in society are felt by all mothers, not only those who work outside of the home. Those who stay home to care for their children feel that society expects them to perform their mothering and housekeeping duties to perfection, to volunteer in their children's school, and to prepare elaborate meals for their families. The fact that they don't work outside of the home only emphasizes their maternal role to the point where they also end up burning out.

In sum, the current dominant discourse of motherhood promotes a set of expectations that are impossible to achieve. Maternal care giving is viewed as essential and central to the "healthy" development of a child. Paradoxically, mothers are offered little support to carry out this endeavour (Hays, 1996). One can conclude that many mothers are consequently left with strong feelings of guilt, inadequacy, and may view themselves as deficient (Eyer, 1996; Seagram and Daniluk, 2002). So much emphasis is put on their relationship with their children in a society that tends to be individualistic and lacks community support, that the exclusivity and isolation of the mother-child relationship becomes problematic for both the mother and the child.

When we examine the dominant discourse, how we got here, and how it impacts mothers, we can develop a better understanding of what it is and how we can resist it. Mothers today are expected to not only be great housekeepers, but also to serve nutritious meals, drive children to many activities, stimulate them, read to them, be empathic, spend quality time with them, and given our culture of fear, to supervise their play at all times (Douglas and Michaels, 2004; Thurer, 1994). The dominant discourse has lead to an unprecedented level of stress for mothers (Warner, 2006). Hays (1996) defines intensive mothering as mothering that is child focused, expert guided, emotionally absorbing, labour intensive, and financially expensive. Is this intensity yielding more evolved children? Is it benefiting mothers or society at large? Mothering that is propelled by this discourse does not guarantee children who will turn out "perfect," with high self-esteem and good mental health, or who are responsible, dedicated, and independent. And yet intensive mothering places mothers who attempt to parent this way at risk of feeling guilty, exhausted, depleted, and with significant self-doubt (Contratto, 1984; Seagram and Daniluk, 2002). Nevertheless, most women keep trying.

Children may not be better off when raised by the dominant discourse of motherhood. As a public speaker, several times a year I am invited to speak to groups of parents in preschools, elementary schools and high schools. In the past several years, I have asked hundreds of parents if they think that teenagers today are better off or doing better than teenagers 25-30 years ago. And I always hear a unanimous "no." Mothers in the past 25-30 years have believed that if they parented intensively, their children would be better equipped to deal with adult life (O'Reilly, 2004). There are many factors such as temperament, level of ability, presence or absence of extended family, media, school experience, societal messages about a variety of issues, life experiences, and social supports that influence our children's development (Douglas and Michaels, 2004; Nelson, 2010). However, mothers believe that if they engage in intensive mothering they can protect their children from all these influences.

By buying into the dominant discourse of motherhood, mothers buy into the belief that they can raise the perfect child if they follow the "right" practices, which also suggests that if the child does not turn out perfect, they are at fault. Mothering intensively may not prevent these children from struggling later in life or protect them from other influences that may lead to later problems. But mothering intensely is depleting and hurting mothers, so no one wins.

I was recently approached by CBC Television (in Canada) requesting that I grant them an interview for a documentary that, as they told me at the time, was exploring why university students seem to be experiencing higher levels of anxiety than in any previous time in history and how the way they were parented impacted them. I clarified with the producer that I would not participate if this documentary was, in any way, going to portray parents in a negative light. I said that I recognized that parents today are certainly very involved in the lives of their children but what was important for the program to clarify was that "experts," the extensive popular parenting literature, and the media (Douglas and Michaels, 2004) were promoting a style of parenting that is intensive, expensive, and over-involved. The producer promised that the program would not be about blaming parents or portraying them in a negative light.

I agreed to be interviewed but when the documentary aired, it showed some parents willing to throw a 40,000 dollar party for their baby's first birthday and others whose twenty-something children went bankrupt because they had been raised to be overconfident about their personal "gifts." The program showed some extreme examples of how the dominant discourse manifests in certain parental practices. However, it did not explain to the viewer that parents are not out to spoil their children, but rather are buying into a series of social messages that promise to benefit their children in the long run. Without the context of why parents are doing so much for their children, the program portrayed mothers as passive victim-like robots of a parenting discourse that is draining and often ineffective. I hope this book will challenge that view and show that mothers can be empowered and actively engage in the process of resistance and choice.

There is plenty of evidence to demonstrate that the dominant discourse of motherhood is hurting and oppressing mothers. This discourse promotes an ideal that is impossible to achieve. What is more, the actual outcome of mothering our children this way is not benefiting our children or mothers themselves. It is time that women find alternative ways to mother. Yet, the power of this discourse holds us back from trying even when we are faced with so many contradictions. Given that the dominant discourse of motherhood promotes motherhood as a natural condition for women, women expect motherhood to be the right choice for them (Boulton, 1983; McMahon, 1995). Because of the false claims it makes, mothers expect motherhood to be joyful and easy. Being a mother, we are told, is an extension of a woman's femininity; it is the way one can be a real woman; by being a mother, a woman is to be fulfilled and happy (Eyer, 1996; Thurer, 1994). But by buying into this ideology, women find themselves experiencing mixed feelings regarding mothering because the ideal and the myths promise one thing and motherhood delivers another one (Boulton, 1983; Maushart, 2000). Because women are told that they will be totally fulfilled by their roles as mothers, they have a difficult time sharing with others the difficulties they encounter in being mothers (Maushart, 2000). A painful realization a mother comes to soon after having her first child is that she must ignore her own desires and needs and she must also soon face the imminent blame if anything goes wrong with her children.

I recently spoke to a mother who confessed that becoming a mother was not at all what she expected; mothering felt like a burden, a prison, and a disappointment. She had become depressed and although she loved her children, she realized that without community and proper supports, mothering became a burden and an isolating experience. She felt intensely guilty for not being happy now that she was home raising her children. She felt guilty every time she felt angry and burdened by her children, every time she wished to be elsewhere rather than with her children. In addition, she felt extremely depressed at the loss of her freedom and lack of personal activities that nurtured her. She couldn't understand why she was not elated with this life. When she chose to stay at home to raise her children, she looked forward to the promised fairy tale of being the loving, patient, and fulfilled mother. And instead, she became so depressed she couldn't see a way out. She is an example of how the false promises of the discourse trap women and deliver pain and exhaustion. So how did we end up here? What were the various factors that led to the development of the dominant discourse of motherhood that has had so many consequences for mothers? In the remainder of this chapter, I attempt to provide a cursory review of the feminist literature that aims to answer these questions.

Factors that Influenced the Development of the Dominant Discourse

The dominant discourse of motherhood is a specific set of messages, statements, terms, and prescriptions for behaviors, thoughts, and feelings that mothers must understand, buy into, and adhere to. This discourse of motherhood attempts to create a common understanding of the proper rules of conduct for mothers (Robinson and Robinson, 1998). The dominant discourse of motherhood operates as a master discourse or hegemonic narrative that attempts to dictate how women must mother (O'Reilly, 2006a, p. 13). It subtly, but forcefully, creates power structures, which place mothers at a disadvantage and with reduced social power. It is pervasive and the model against which all mothering practices are measured. This dominant discourse gives mothers a "powerless responsibility" to care for children (Rich, 1986). It puts mothers in a position where they are given all the responsibility for their children but very little power to define their lives. It does not allow them the agency to call the shots, so to speak. The dominant discourse forces mothers to live by the values of a patriarchal society that oppresses them, rather than by their own values. As Sara Ruddick suggests, mothers are mothering under the watchful eye of others, which leads mothers to lose confidence in their own authority to mother as they see fit (O'Reilly, 2006a; Ruddick, 1983).

Adrienne Rich exposes motherhood as a social institution that oppresses and controls women (1986). She writes of the demands, physical labor, and emotional strain of motherhood. At the same time, Rich distinguishes between the love and commitment mothers experience for their children and the institution of motherhood that proposes a set of expectations that are unfair and patriarchal. The discourse categorizes women as good mothers when they live by this ideal and as bad mothers when they deviate from it. The dominant discourse suggests that motherhood is fulfilling and always rewarding. It promises that motherhood is the most important and best thing a woman can do. But there is a catch: there is only one way to do it right and if a mother does not follow this prescribed model, she is deemed a bad mother. This discourse tortures mothers with the idea that if they do not love everything about being a mother there is something wrong with them (Douglas and Michaels, 2004).

Many have written about and discussed this discourse (Douglas and Michaels, 2004; Hays, 1996; Maushart, 2000; O'Brien Hallstein, 2006; O'Reilly, 2004, 2006a, 2011; Thurer, 1994). For example, Douglas and Michaels describe the discourse as the "new momism," which is "the insistence that no woman is truly complete or fulfilled unless she has kids, that women remain the best primary caretakers of children, and that to be a remotely decent mother, a woman has to devote her entire physical, psychological, emotional, and intellectual being 24/7, to her children" (2004, p. 4). This set of ideals appears to celebrate motherhood but in reality it promulgates a set of standards of perfection that are impossible to achieve (O'Brien Hallstein, 2006). So how does such a powerful discourse evolve?

Most models of motherhood have historically developed in response to changing social and economic factors (O'Reilly, 2004). In other words, the expectations on mothers evolve from social reorganization particularly related to gender roles and behaviour. Examples of this can be found in the eras of the Industrial Revolution and World War II (Hays, 1996; O'Reilly, 2004; Thurer, 1994). The current image of the stay-at-home mother began to take shape as a result of the Industrial Revolution. Industrialization transformed family life from one where families worked collectively as a family to produce their sustenance to one where economic work was removed from the home. This created a model where the domestic space was now an "exclusively nonproductive and private realm" (O'Reilly, 2004, p. 5). Furthermore, during the Industrial Revolution the division of the public and private spheres became gender specific. It was men who left the home to work in factories and women who remained in the home to care for children. In other words, men belonged in the public sphere and women to the private domain where they were to serve as the decorative wife or the "Angel of the House" (O'Reilly, 2010; Thurer, 1994). This division led to the idea that stay-at-home motherhood is the "natural" and necessary place for a mother. Mothers were now left to run the home and care for their children on their own. The idea that mothers belong at home began to be seen as the ideal model of motherhood.

In addition to the Industrial Revolution, another period that significantly restructured gender roles occurred during the Second World War. During the War, mothers were invited to take the jobs that men who went off to war had left behind. Mothers who worked were offered daycare for their children and were celebrated for contributing to their country (O'Reilly, 2006a; Thurer, 1994). However, after the War, in the interest of economic growth in the United States and Canada, mothers were forced to free up their jobs for men returning from the War (Hays, 1996; Gleason, 1999). Motherhood, they were told, was more important than paid employment (Hays, 1996; O'Reilly, 2006a). In order to create this social change, those with political, social, and economic power supported a discourse that redesigned what constituted good motherhood: wherein mothers belonged in the home. During this period mothers were promoted as the central caregivers of children; they were told that they were biologically the rightful parent to care and nurture children. It was, in fact, during the post-World War II period that the theory of attachment was first publicized (Arnup, 1994; Thurer, 1994). It promoted the belief that children need constant mothering and that those that do not experience constant, safe, and close attachments to their mothers will forever be damaged (Bowlby, 1991).

The current dominant discourse of motherhood began to take shape after the Second World War. However, expectations that mothers should spend a lot of quality time with their children, purchase all gadgets necessary for children, keep the child always in sight, and be closely involved and empathic at all times evolved during the late 1970s and '80s (O'Reilly, 2004). The post-war expectations on mothers, on the other hand, were more about domesticity rather than about spending quality time with, and personal and emotional energy on, children (Hays, 1996; O'Reilly, 2004; 2006a; Thurer, 1994). Andrea O'Reilly refers to this Post-war model as "custodial motherhood" (2004, p. 7). Post-War mothers were expected to be around but not to practice intensive mothering as we know it today. Custodial mothering was about being *home* but not necessarily being *with* children all the time. She describes a culture where children spent their time out in the neighborhood playing with other children and amusing themselves; they rarely looked to their mothers for entertainment. Mothers did not spend their afternoons and weekends driving children to a myriad of activities as they do today. O'Reilly suggests that this model lasted from 1946 to about the mid-1970s.

Various factors that occurred after the 1970s have contributed to the current dominant discourse of motherhood. Some of these factors include: a backlash to feminism; women having fewer children and entering the labor force in record numbers; women postponing children until they established their career; consumerism/materialism; neoliberalism; the culture of fear; and the power of "expert" advice and psychological theories. In examining each of these factors, we can begin to deconstruct the basis upon which the current dominant discourse of motherhood is predicated.

The women's movement of the 1970s sought to achieve equality for women in the areas of education, work, and social power. Feminists at the time believed that women should have equal access to jobs and education that were usually reserved for men. Their aim was to increase choices for women and to liberate them from patriarchal oppression (Douglas and Michaels, 2004; Greer, 1972; Porter, 2010) and to improve the social position of women and mothers. They hoped to generate financial independence for women, and to be more than a housewife dependent on and at the mercy of her husband. They spread their message through the practice of consciousness-raising. Consciousness-raising was a powerful movement; women gathered in living rooms and wherever they could to discuss and change their disempowered position in society.

This movement influenced many people in different parts of the world, and some improvements gradually emerged, at least for middle-class woman. However, one consequence of this movement was that motherhood for the middle-class mother was seen by some circles as getting in the way of women gaining equality and independence from men's control (Douglas and Michaels, 2004). Feminists in the '70s sought to make parenting more equal between men and women. They named the elephant in the room for mothers: motherhood was a prison from which women should escape and into which they should refuse to be trapped (Douglas and Michaels, 2004).

Baby boom women in the '70s wanted to break down the barriers of the male dominated labor force and, as a result, became overachievers to prove that they were not stupid, hysterical, irrational, and flighty (Douglas and Michael, 2004). They then brought this overachieving attitude to motherhood. Many women also interpreted this fight for equality as having to live by a male lifestyle. "Motherhood did not fit easily into this way of life and many feminist mothers saw feminist theory as opposed to motherhood" (Porter, 2010, p. 11).

In the next two decades, women made gains in the areas of employment and education. And yet, the division of labor in the home remained unchanged. Working mothers continued to be responsible for most of their children's care and domestic work, as they do today. They were expected to be responsible for domestic tasks. Yet, this did not stop them from making progress in the public realm through employment and education. The equality women gained threatened a patriarchal society that is set up for men to be in charge and to hold all the social and political control. It wasn't long before a backlash occurred.

The current dominant discourse of motherhood is a backlash discourse (Douglas and Michaels, 2004; O'Reilly, 2004; Porter, 2010). Patriarchal structures resisted the true liberation of women. Allowing women social and possibly political power became too dangerous for the status quo where men control economic and political interests. Promoting a discourse that distracts and pressures mothers to focus on their children is one sure way to stop the progress women can make. O'Reilly (2004) explains that this new discourse was a backlash to women's increased participation in the labor force and in previously male-dominated professions:

> It seems that just as women were making inroads and feeling confident, a new discourse of motherhood emerged, which made two things inevitable: that women would forever feel inadequate as mothers, and that work and motherhood would be forever seen as in conflict and incompatible. I believe that the guilt and shame women experience in failing to live up to what is, in fact, an impossible ideal is neither accidental nor inconsequential. Rather it is deliberately manufactured and monitored. (p. 10)

Although the discourse is impossible to achieve, many mothers still continue to try. Many working mothers, who buy into the belief that achieving the ideal is possible if they devote themselves to their children, have quit their jobs. So it is no surprise that the current dominant discourse of motherhood began to take force and conquer our psyche, as mothers entered the workforce (Douglas and Michaels, 2004, p. 11). The discourse led mothers to be caught between two powerful forces: either to have a career and be financially self-sufficient or be a devoted, present mother. Their sense of accomplishment in the public arena through their work outside of the home and their education gradually became destabilized by the "chronic ambivalence" they experienced because of the morality of their choices and the question of how adequate their mothering was (Gross, 1998). This new dominant discourse sought "to contain and, where possible, eradicate all of the social changes brought on by feminism" (Douglas and Michaels, 2004, p. 23). The power behind this discourse is that it aims to question the motivations of mothers where they are most vulnerable: in the love for their children.

This backlash has been justified by what has come to be called Postfeminism (Douglas and Michaels, 2004, p. 24), which puts forth the idea that we have reached equality between the sexes and that feminism is therefore no longer needed. Douglas and Michaels suggest that it goes something like this: now that women are "equal" they can work outside the home in previously male dominated jobs, have their own credit rating and bank accounts, and also be empathic, nurturing, and the devoted, selfless mother. Postfeminism has been the newest attempt at re-domesticating women and it does it through the dominant discourse of mother-hood. Douglas and Michaels do a great job at providing a narrative that illustrates this well:

> Here is the progression: Feminism won; you can have it all; of course you want children; mothers are better at raising children than fathers; of course children come first; of course you come last; today's children need constant attention, cultivation, and adoration, or they'll become failures and hate you forever; you don't want to fail at that; it's easier for mothers to abandon their work and their dreams than for fathers; you don't want it all anymore (which is good because you can't have it all); who cares about equality, you're too tired; and whoops—here we are in 1954. (2004, p. 25)

I recently taught a feminist course entitled Gender and Sex Role Issues in Counselling. Many of the students, who were all female, confessed at the beginning of the course that they were reluctant to see themselves as feminist. They believed that feminism was anti-man and anti-feminine. They were willing to take a class on this topic, but they were not willing to call themselves feminist. The majority of the students were in their late 20s and early 30s. I think this is an example of the backlash to feminism where media has portrayed feminism in such a way that it has misinformed many. This has opened the door to create a backlash discourse that creates the perfect conditions to promote a discourse of motherhood that sells mothers the idea that they belong in the home with their children. I am happy to say that all the students changed their minds about feminism by the end of the course. They developed a clearer understanding of what feminism is about and emerged as feminists with strong convictions. There is enough evidence that women are still oppressed by various discourses and institutions to demonstrate that the falsehood in the belief that feminism is no longer needed. Within this feminist discourse alone, much research suggests the oppression inherent in the ways that mothers aspire to live by the ideal of the perfect mother (Boulton, 1983; Garey, 1995; Stoppard, 2000).

The dominant discourse suggests to mothers that if they are enlightened, they will choose to stay home with their children (Douglas and Michaels, 2004). The middle class mother of the '50s stayed home because she had no choice; the middle class mother of today has the choice but she wants to be there for her kids because, as the discourse demands, mothers are the best caregivers for their children (O'Reilly, 2004). Middle-class women after the '70s postponed motherhood until they established a career (Douglas and Michaels, 2004; O'Reilly, 2004). Women who were busy breaking down the barriers of the male dominated world of work, and who had postponed having children in the '70s, began having children in the '80s. The current discourse that contains the expectation of intensive mothering emerged and gained significance in the '80s. Those women who postponed having children until they had established their careers, translated the rat race of building their careers into their mothering by engaging in a lot of activities to prove their productivity (Douglas and Michaels, 2004; O'Reilly, 2004). The discourse suggests that a successful woman could be the same superwoman at home that she was at work (Douglas and Michaels, 2004). The professional working mother who is away from her child during the day practices intensive mothering on evenings and weekends as a way of compensating for her time away from the children (O'Reilly, 2004).

In addition, the introduction of more effective methods of contraception not only allowed women to postpone motherhood until they established their careers, but also to have fewer children (Thurer, 1994). The discourse then suggested that now that she had fewer children and modern technology to ease the burden of housework and career, mothers could devote all freed time to their children (Douglas and Michaels, 2004; O'Reilly, 2004). This model of maternal practice gradually became very different from the custodial mothering model of the 1950s and '60s. The modern mother was now expected to focus all her physical, emotional, and financial energy on her children (Hays, 1996). Her children were the center of her universe and her most important life project (Douglas and Michaels, 2004; Hays, 1996). She was to love them unconditionally and develop strong deep attachments to them.

The idea that attachment is crucial and that mothers should be mindful of developing strong, secure attachments with their children is central to the dominant discourse of motherhood (Douglas and Michaels, 2004; Hays, 1996; O'Reilly, 2004, 2006a). Good mothering, they are told, begins in the womb; mothers are expected to play music to their womb and plan a delivery that is warm and caring. The first moments after birth are also crucial in the future of the baby. Mothers are expected to hold their babies and put them to the breast right after birth. It was in the 1980s that this theory of attachment really took force and led to sacrificial motherhood. Mothers were told that attachment and bonding right after birth and throughout childhood was essential to healthy development (Bowlby, 1991). Experts told mothers that they must bond and pay close attention to their children (Arnup, 1994). In addition, and to make matter worse, mothers were threatened with serious consequences if they did not get it right. They would be blamed if their children developed any later problems. The good mother was now the one who loved her children unconditionally, was always available to her children, and was involved in every facet of their lives (Porter, 2010). Gradually, mothers were called to become increasingly involved in their children's lives and to be present not only in the home but also to spend as much time as possible loving, stimulating, attending to, serving, and catering to their children (Porter, 2010). They were expected to purchase all the necessary goods and items to provide "the right" stimulation and environment for their kids (Hays, 1996). The capitalistic agenda was behind this added pressure on mothers.

Consumerism and capitalism have also contributed to the evolution of the dominant discourse of motherhood. After the Second World War, both the U.S. and Canada planned to become global economic powers. In order to achieve this goal, they needed to transform their hard working and hard saving citizens into consumers of goods (Cushman, 1995). The way they achieved this was by convincing citizens that happiness was found in the purchasing of homes, cars, televisions, clothing, appliances, and educational toys, for example (Cushman, 1995). Mothers were encouraged to purchase baby and child products that promised better parenting and healthier children (Hays, 1996). Most of the advertising in newspapers and magazines suggested that purchasing educational toys, dolls, nice baby clothes, hygienic products, and safe baby furniture was an important aspect of good mothering (Arnup, 1994; Douglas and Michaels, 2004; Thurer, 1994.) Mothers were told that with the right workshop, book, and expert advice they could learn the perfect way to make their babies happy. This ideology of consumerism that promised answers to every challenge resulted in an unprecedented degree of pressure for mothers. Most mothers maintain this standard, resulting in feelings of inadequacy. And this has had many consequences on mothers, children and society.

The dominant Western discourse of motherhood has also thrived because of an individualistic social structure that isolates a mother within a single-family home where she must acquire all the necessary goods to run her home and raise her children in isolation from other mothers and families. In countries like the U.S. and Canada, reformers, governments, and those with economic interests needed to encourage independent family units that would become consumers in the '50s, '60s, and '70s (Gleason, 1999). Within this family unit, it was important to raise children who could become independent, tax paying, consuming citizens as this would support a growing economy. Notice how in the U.S. and Canada, young people were expected to leave home and become independent at an early age as opposed to other countries in the world. Parents, therefore, were told that it was important to promote self-control and independence in their children. Many of these needs were put forward as universal. Parents were promised that if they raised their children this way, *all* children would turn out to be successful. These beliefs have gradually become part of North American society's core values.

So, in the 1970s women became "a market" (Douglas and Michaels, 2004, p. 11; Gleason, 1999). Marketing campaigns to sell them items such as make-up, household appliances, children's products, and clothing became the norm in women's magazines, newspapers, and television ads. Increased emphasis on child safety was marketed in many magazines, newscasts, and parenting advice literature. The good mother had to buy these products to protect, educate, stimulate, indulge her kids, and to be a good mother. Materialism had become something to aspire to.

After the late '70s and '80s, middle class women who worked outside of the home and generated an income were now in a position to purchase the many products they were marketed as essential (O'Reilly, 2004). Mothers are the main consumer of items for children. And today's middle class working mother has buying power; she can spend her money in purchasing everything that promises happy babies and children and the social identity of the good mother (O'Reilly, 2004).

The modern dominant discourse of motherhood places all responsibility on mothers to provide for, protect, care, and raise children. This differs from old models of maternal practice that involved communities and joint community responsibility for the care of children. This aspect of the discourse was influenced by the emergence of neo-liberalism and the free market ideology (Douglas and Michaels, 2004). Neo-liberalism, as it has come to be known, also played a part in the emergence of aspects of the modern dominant discourse of motherhood. As Simon-Kumar puts it: "Neo-liberalism, which is based on the free-market principles of the 1980s and 1990s ignores the relevance of mothering within its discourse of cost-effective society. Yet, ironically, it is women's mothering and caring roles that pick up the gaps in social services that are no longer funded by the state" (2009, p.143). There is research to suggest that women's work in the private sphere, particularly in mothering, increases in direct response to fewer government-funded social and community services (Simon-Kumar, 2009).

To put it simply, the neoliberal "free market" ideology has produced a social ethos that prioritizes "productivity" and "efficiency" (Vandenbeld Giles, 2011). In the name of productivity and economic efficiency, neoliberalism seeks to transfer responsibility for the economy from the public to the private sphere, with governments assigning responsibility for services and supports for families to the private sphere and, in many cases, the family itself.

Therefore, those who can afford services can access them, but those who cannot have to fill in the gaps left behind by services privatization and cutbacks themselves (Douglas and Michaels, 2004; Simon-Kumar, 2009). For example, without universal daycare, an employed mother must pay for daycare or stay home to provide the care herself. The discourse proposes a list of duties that are needed to raise children properly. But it doesn't only proscribe a list of duties and expectations; it tells mothers that *they* must provide the child with all that is needed. In this way, it releases governments and society as a whole from any responsibility for the care of children.

As a public speaker, I often ask parents what is most overwhelming about being a parent. Always mentioned is that when they were kids in the 1960s, '70s, or early '80s, they could just go out and play in the neighborhood or park. They tell me that in the summer they would be out all day and their mother would tell them to come back at dinnertime. But the streets are no longer seen as safe. These parents also explain that when they were kids, they walked to get to school, but today children must be driven to and from school because it is not safe. There are too many dangers, they tell me, like the possibility of abduction or of pedophiles lurking. I have heard how the dangers on the streets have taken away the fun of playing outside. Neighborhoods are just not safe anymore, they say. Susan Douglas and Meredith Michaels wrote about this extensively in their book, *The Mommy Myth* (2004). They point to the exaggerated dangers of razor blades in Halloween candy, the molesters in daycare centers, child abductions, children's clothing that catches on fire, toys that choke children, stalkers, harmful over the counter medications for children, and more. Increasingly since the early 1980s, mothers have been warned about all the dangers that can harm their children.

Again, this might be a backlash to feminism's progress. Just when women were willing to leave the home to work and be financially independent, a series of messages emerge that tell mothers that their children are fragile and in danger, and that mothers need to be ever vigilant in order to protect their children. We live in a culture of fear; we are told that there are dangers on the streets, in our food, in the chemicals in our plastics, or on the Internet (Glassner,

1999). Mothers must attend to their child's safety (Douglas and Michaels, 2004). Mothers must teach their children about the potential of abuse without scaring them.

This culture of fear has made the dominant discourse of motherhood one where mothers must not only be present and cater to their children, they must not let them out of their sight. So here is the formula to derail the progress women had achieved through the feminist movement: children need safe and secure attachments, mothers are the best caregivers, there are serious dangers both inside and outside the home, mothers are the best protectors of children. When mothers fail to meet their children's needs based on these "facts," children can be molested, hurt, kidnapped, or grow up to be addicts, criminals, mentally ill, poorly adjusted, or dependent. As Douglas and Michaels put it "a woman's need or desire to work [is] constantly pitted against the safety and healthy development of her kids" (p. 107).

One of the most significant changes in maternal practice has been to shift the "know-how" and expertise about how to mother from mothers and grandmothers to "experts." The twentieth century saw the beginning of a science/expert discourse that told mothers that scientists and experts were to be consulted for scientific- and research-based knowledge on how to raise children. An important social phenomenon of the twentieth century was the belief that science had the answers to many questions previously unanswered and the solution to many previously difficult tasks (Arnup, 1994). This phenomenon impacted the dominant discourse of motherhood by stating that maternal instinct was no longer sufficient; mothers had to refer to experts to discover the best way to care for their children. Psychologically, this impacted mothers by stripping their self-confidence.

In the twentieth century, the advice literature placed mothers as the sole caretakers of children and encouraged them to remain at home while avoiding paid employment (Arnup, 1994; Bowlby, 1991; Gleason, 1997). Moral reformers who belonged to the white middle class included professionals such as psychologists, social workers, writers, and politicians. Their access to social power enabled them to promote a particular model of mothering. Many of these so-called experts assigned a Freudian view to mothering wherein the first five years of life have the most impact on the development of personality and adult behavior, placing mothers as solely responsible for the future mental health of children (Arnup, 1994). The dominant discourse was certainly affirmed and legitimized for North American culture by "experts" such as Benjamin Spock, T. Berry Brazelton, and Penelope Leach (Gross, 1998). Spock's book, *Baby and Child Care* (1946), became the bible for mothers in the late '40s, '50s, and beyond. Spock combined psychoanalytic theory, stage theories, and child-centered approaches to offer advice on how to respond appropriately to each child based on the child's developmental stage and all of the child's needs. He told mothers that maternal affection was key and that a mother must allow her child the space to express his or her needs. Providing this care would be a pleasant and pleasurable experience because children are inherently good and friendly and mothers are naturally empathic and loving. Spock warned against mothers working outside the home. He was a proponent of "quality time" and suggested that mothers should develop strong relationships with their children; being present was essential for this to occur. He spoke of the necessity of bonding with the infant at birth.

In addition to pediatricians like Spock, experts in the field of psychology were also central to the spread of the current ideology of children and their needs. The discipline of psychology saw an opportunity to establish itself as a prestigious and necessary science (Arnup, 1994). Psychologists began to teach parents the best way to raise successful, high functioning children based on "scientific" data that dictated how children develop and how parents should contribute to this development (Arnup, 1994; Gleason, 1999). And so, they went to task. Psychologists both in the U.S. and Canada advanced a series of theories about children and parenting. In addition to Bowlby's theory of attachment, B.F. Skinner in the 1950s told parents that behaviour was the result of external causes (1953). Skinner told parents that children behave as they do because of positive or negative reinforcement. Jean Piaget (1952; 1960) also advanced his stage theory of cognitive development, which was later to become the basis for the idea that if parents provide mental stimulation for their children, they can improve their intelligence. His theory was then used as proof that children had specific needs and capacities at different ages. When taken together, these theories appear to suggest that children were malleable and impressionable, which meant that parents should proceed with caution and educate themselves in order to provide the best environment, stimulation, love, guidance, and gentle discipline for their children.

It has always been the case that those who seek to "revolutionize" motherhood belong to the white middle class. Economists, politicians, health professionals, and reformers have historically been predominantly white, middle-class males. The dominant discourse is based on a white, middle class, educated, heterosexual, married philosophy (Douglas and Michaels, 2004; Fox, 2006). It does not consider diversity, different levels of education, or financial resources. The dominant discourse dictates that mothers must practice intensive mothering regardless of their background and resources. And yet, maternal practices are influenced by a mother's financial and social resources.

There is evidence that there is a relationship between financial and social resources and mothering practices (Duncan, 2005). Duncan posits, for example, that working class mothers tend to concentrate on helping their kids navigate and survive disadvantages and challenges which is traditionally not the case with middle-class mothers. Working class parents tend to be more concerned about teaching their kids the tools and strength to cope with the instability, injustice, and hardship that is characteristic of their lives (Duncan, 2005). This suggests that mothering is a classed activity. Yet, these mothers may be judged by the middle-class ideal to be bad mothers.

Mothers and their partners, if they have one, are given full responsibility for meeting the basic subsistence needs of children (Fox, 2006). In order to raise a child, women are now expected to spend a great deal of emotional and physical energy caring for their children. And yet, mothers care for children in different conditions with "varying social, emotional, and material resources" (Fox, 2006, p. 237). The dominant discourse of motherhood may only be accessible to those mothers that are middle class and who have the resources to stay at home or pay for daycare if they are employed. It is this middle class mother who is more likely to be able to purchase what is expected to do it right, and to have the financial stability that allows her to be patient, caring, attentive, and a chauffeur. In order to stay home, a mother, in most cases, needs to be free of economic pressures and financial struggles which can lead her to go back into the workforce (Fox, 2006). Fox found in her qualitative study of 40 heterosexual couples and one single mother that having financial security was central to being able to provide the huge amounts of energy, patience, and mental and physical resources that are needed to attempt to live up to the ideal of intensive mothering. Middle class mothers may come the closest to living by the discourse, although given that it is impossible to achieve, they still end up feeling anxious, deficient, and guilty.

Mothers from other societal groups may not be able to set their lives up to live up to or even attempt to live by this ideal. These are the mothers who are often seen as bad or deviant mothers. "Women's social class, ethnicity, culture, and sexual orientation restrict the strategies and meanings that can fashion their mothering experiences" (Medina and Magnuson, 2009, p. 91). For example, mothers who are on social assistance are set up by the discourse as the most deviant of all mothers (Douglas and Michaels, 2004; Medina and Magnuson, 2009), and therefore if you are not able to devote the time, money, patience, and dedication to your kids, you should not have any.

On the flip side, one can also ask if resistance is only possible by those with resources. My study may not answer this question. The 15 women I interviewed were all white and with various levels of post-secondary education (I will provide a detailed description of the participants' demographics in Chapter 3). One who was 23, and who was in the lower-income bracket, was in her second semester at a community college. Yearly income levels among the participants varied from $30,000 (CAD) to over $75,000 (CAD). One of the partnered mothers who stayed at home, had a Bachelor's degree, and yet her yearly family income was in the $30,000 (CAD) range for a family of four. She lived in a small basement suite with her husband and two children. We need more research that examines the lives of women from various economic backgrounds, sexual orientations, educational levels, ethnicities, and so on. Amy Middleton suggests that mothering under duress may not allow mothers to practice empowered mothering (2006). She asks, is empowered mothering only for those who are financially and educationally well endowed? She explains, "mothers who live in difficult relational, financial, and social circumstances are restricted from achieving states of agency, autonomy, authenticity and this may prevent them from engaging in practices of feminist mothering" (p. 72).

In closing, the current dominant discourse of motherhood expects mothers to be fully responsible for the physical, spiritual, and psychological well being of their children (Douglas and Michaels, 2004; Gleason, 1999; Hays, 1996; Thurer, 1994). It expects mothers to communicate empathy and understanding toward their children. In addition, this discourse promotes the idea that mothers should be ever-present, sacrificial, and loving. Mothers are told they are the best caregivers for their children and that it is crucial for them to develop strong attachments with their children. At the same time, they must exercise care in not overdoing their attachment so as to not raise dependent children.

What is more, the dominant discourse of motherhood emphasizes that a child's needs always come before those of his or her mother. If something goes wrong with children, it is the mother who is to blame. In addition, in order to help themselves parent correctly, mothers are expected to consult experts. Mothers are told that if they do not parent correctly, they may raise children into adults who will develop mental health issues or addictions. Finally, the dominant discourse of the successful woman complicates matters for mothers because it leads them to feel torn between their obligations at home and at work.

This dominant discourse has led mothers to be fully immersed in sacrificing more and more of their freedom, needs, interests, money, and psychological well-being. As Judith Warner states in her book *Perfect Madness* (2006), parents today live under an intense anxiety that is unprecedented. She explains that the list of expectations on mothers is impossible to achieve. And yet, the on-going attempts to live by this ideal are leading mothers to struggle with high levels of stress and anxiety. As Bonnie Fox posits, "In recent decades, expectations about the work needed to raise a child successfully have escalated at a dizzying rate: the bar is now sky-high" (2006, p. 236). The pressure created by this discourse will be fully expanded in the next chapter.

Chapter 2

The Experience of Mothering Under the Cloud of the Dominant Discourse of Motherhood

WOULD YOU APPLY? MOTHER'S JOB PERMANENT; worth its weight in jewel*s*.

Position: Mom, Mama, Mommy, Ma, Mother.

Job Description: Long term, team players needed for challenging permanent work in an often chaotic environment. Candidates must possess excellent communication and organizational skills and be willing to work variable hours, which will include evenings and weekends and frequent 24-hour shifts on call. Some overnight travel required, including trips to primitive camping sites on rainy weekends and endless sports tournaments in faraway cities. Travel expenses not reimbursed. Extensive courier duties also required.

Responsibilities: The rest of your life.

Must be willing to be hated, at least temporarily, until someone needs $5. Must be willing to bite tongue repeatedly. Also must possess the physical stamina of a pack mule and be able to go from zero to 60 km/h in three seconds flat in case, this time, the screams from the backyard are not someone crying wolf.

Must be willing to face stimulating technical challenges, such small gadget repairs, mysteriously sluggish toilets, and stuck zippers. Must screen phone calls, maintain calendars, and coordinate production of multiple homework projects.

Must have ability to plan and organize social gatherings for clients of all ages and mental outlooks.

Must be willing to be indispensable one minute, an embarrassment the next.

Must handle assembly and product safety testing of a half million cheap, plastic toys and battery-operated devices.

Must always hope for the best but be prepared for the worst.

Must assume final, complete accountability for the quality of the end product.

Responsibilities also include floor maintenance and janitorial work throughout the facility.

Possibility for Advancement and Promotion: Virtually none. Your job is to remain in the same position for years, without complaining, and constantly retraining and updating your skills, so that those in your charge can ultimately surpass you.

Previous experience: None required, unfortunately. On-the-job training offered on a continually exhausting basis.

Wages and Compensation: Get this: You pay them, offering frequent raises and bonuses. A balloon payment is due when they turn 18 because of the assumption that college will help them become financially independent. When you die, you give them whatever is left. The oddest thing about this reverse-salary scheme is that you actually enjoy it and wish you could only do more.

Benefits: While no health or dental insurance, pension, tuition reimbursement, paid holidays or stock options are offered, this job supplies limitless opportunities for personal growth and free hugs for life if you play your cards right.
(*Tri-City News* Coquitlam, BC, May 8, 2004, p. 20)

The current dominant discourse of motherhood promotes a set of expectations that are impossible to achieve. Maternal caregiving is viewed as essential and central to healthy child development. Paradoxically, mothers are offered little support to carry out this endeavor and yet most of them are practicing intensive mothering, which is demanding of their time, energy, and well-being. One can conclude that many mothers are consequently left with strong feelings of guilt, inadequacy, and deficiency (Seagram and Daniluk, 2002). Much emphasis is put on their relationship with their children in an individualistic society lacking in community support, resulting in an isolating mother-child relationship. Regardless of whether mothers are employed or at home, they appear to be impacted by the expectations set forth by the dominant discourse and the multiple roles—mother, employee, wife, and so on—that influence them. In the end, how and how much does this discourse impact the wellbeing of mothers? To answer this question, we now turn our exploration to the struggles that mothers experience when carrying out multiple roles, the impact of the discourse on them, and how some mothers have attempted to resist these expectations. Following this discussion is a summary of various research studies and a review of some of the literature that has focused on these aspects.

Maintaining the Identity of the Full-time Mother

Most mothers today find themselves juggling two or more roles at once. The roles of mother and employee appear to be the most significant for most mothers (Hays, 1996; Polasky and Holahan, 1998). Many women appear to believe that the burdens and expectations placed on them are the norm. Therefore, mothers often find ways to accommodate the demands of various roles (Gilbert, Holahan, and Manning, 1981; Polasky and Holahan, 1998). For example, some mothers may redefine role demands and involve others in fulfilling those demands, or they may attempt to meet the various role demands by increasing the levels of energy, time, and commitment. Furthermore, some research suggests that some women will juggle their time in order to maintain their identity as good mothers (Garey, 1995; Krause and Geyer-Pestello, 1985). In other words, because being at home with their children is so important, some mothers will rearrange their schedule in order to maintain their identity as good mothers. For these women, the role of mother takes precedence over their role of worker. This places them at risk of high stress given that they try to fulfill the role of the full-time mother when in reality they are employed outside of the home.

Seeing themselves as good mothers is very important to most women; this often leads them to rearrange their lives and work schedules in order to be with their children as much as possible. In some cases, women will choose professions or employment that allow them to work through the night so that they can be home during the day. Researcher Anita Garey (1995) explored the experiences of a group of working mothers in a hospital setting. She sought to discover the strategies they used in order to see themselves as stay-at-home mothers. She found that the mothers she studied used night shift work to de-emphasize their employment status and to make their identities as mothers more highly visible. In other words, the mothers in this study emphasized their identities as stay-at-home mothers by being at work at night and being at home during the day.

This is not uncommon. Many women make amazing efforts to be home as much as possible even if it means being sleep deprived and fatigued, being alienated from the professional aspect of their careers, and lacking time with partners. Anita Garey's research reflects the reality of many mothers who are willing to sacrifice their own well-being to be ever-present. Of course, one can expect to be sleep deprived with an infant because the infant needs care through the night. But is it necessary to continue to put the child's needs—or wants—always ahead of one's own? It seems that this discourse pins mothers into a black and white narrative, where they must choose between being either selfless or selfish. There does not seem to be space for a mother to love her children while also being allowed to practice self-love.

Mothers who choose to work night shifts are an example of the sacrificial mother. By working the night shift, they disguise the fact that they work by hiding its visibility. By working at night, they are able to perform the duties of a stay-at-home mother who is available to her children while maintaining social acceptance in that they uphold their position as stay-at-home mothers. These women are an example of women who try to live up to the ideal of the perfect mother even if means being ever sleep deprived. Most mothers do sacrifice their own self-care to different degrees. And if for any reason they don't, they often feel guilty.

The Reality of Practicing Intensive Mothering

Even though most mothers attempt to reach the ideal, they rarely experience motherhood in a way that reflects the joyful picture of the perfect mother (Boulton, 1983; Hays, 1996; McMahon, 1995). Mothering is about loving and caring for children but this process is often affected by the stress of meeting the expectations of the dominant discourse of motherhood (Bernard, 1974; Rich, 1986). The tension between these two forces leads mothers to experience strain that is inconsistent with the fantasy of the happy mother.

The reality of being a mother does not only involve joy, but also distress, resentment, confusion, anger, and frustration (Maushart, 2000). These aspects of motherhood appear to be silenced by a societal myth that promotes the idea that being a mother is always a fulfilling and beautiful experience. Yet, as mothers know but are reluctant to say out loud, being a mother has many tones, and many ups and downs. Psychologists and sociologists have found that mothers indeed have many experiences that range from joy to pain (Boulton, 1983; Maushart, 2000).

Mary Boulton explored the experiences of motherhood for a group of women in England and the differences in the experience of working-class and middle-class mothers (1983). She found that more than half of the women she interviewed felt irritated while performing their mothering duties. Furthermore, over half of the working-class mothers in her study said they did not derive a sense of meaning from being mothers. She found that only 40 percent of the women in her study were satisfied with their role as mothers and as many as 50 percent were either in conflict with the role or felt distant from it.

The discourse forbids mothers from openly expressing these types of feelings, and we therefore hear so rarely about them. Yet many women secretly suffer not only because of these feelings but also because they feel guilty for experiencing them. Boulton's study reveals that the experience of mothering is not always positive. This is important to note, given that the current dominant beliefs about mothering suggest that motherhood is *always* a fulfilling and positive experience. What is most frustrating is that we collectively know that motherhood is not rosy (Maushart, 2000). And yet most mothers avoid voicing that there are aspects of their experiences of mothering that they dislike. Mothers are not allowed to acknowledge that sometimes they don't like their kids, or that they hate having to be nice all the time or not having time for themselves, or the myriad other concerns they have with their role as mother. Furthermore, society often silences mothers from voicing the negative aspects of their mothering experiences because speaking out could not only be harmful to children but also to their own self-image. In the end, most mothers suffer in silence, which may be why the highest incidence of depression for women happens during their child-bearing and child-rearing years, a tendency to be further explored later.

The reality for many women is that they do not always enjoy mothering and that it can be frustrating, isolating, and conflicted. Most mothers find that some aspects of mothering are very rewarding and others very difficult, as Martha McMahon found in her 1995 study. She explored the meaning that women give to motherhood and identified what mothers see as the rewards and costs of having children. While finding motherhood rewarding by seeing their children grow and learn and by being close to them, the women in her sample reported that the worst features of being a mother for them were the burden and responsibility they experienced. Sadly, this reality is rarely described.

Studies like Boulton's and McMahon's begin to paint a picture of maternal experience under the influence of the dominant discourse of motherhood. They alert us to the complexity of factors that influence a woman's experience of motherhood. Furthermore, they suggest that women do not always enjoy mothering and that mothering can be tough and not always the lovely experience that the ideal portrays. The questions then become, why do mothers struggle? And, are these struggles necessary? Which struggles are created by this ideal and which are just part of the process of raising children? These questions can help us discern ways for mothers to feel empowered through their roles as mothers.

Guilt

Mothers live under such pressure to be perfect mothers that they end up facing some significant consequences. For example, many think that feeling guilty just comes with the job of mothering (Eyer, 1996; Seagram and Daniluk, 2002). Many question themselves and their mothering and feel as though they are failing in one way or another. Many writers and researchers have suggested that guilt has often been reported as a common experience in the lives of mothers (Eyer, 1996; Gordon, 1990; Hays, 1996; Seagram and Daniluk, 2002). For instance, Samantha Seagram and Judith Daniluk at the University of British Columbia carried out a study that explored the meaning and lived experience of maternal guilt for women who had preadolescent children. Their study suggests that mothers experience feelings of complete responsibility toward their children, depletion, inadequacy, fear that their children could be harmed, desire to positively influence their children, profound connection, and loss. This suggests how some mothers feel it is up to them to meet their children's needs and often do not trust others to nurture or contribute to their children's development.

Jill Walls (2010) at the University of North Carolina at Greensboro researched the experience of employed mothers who hold beliefs of intensive mothering. She found that those mothers who bought into the dominant discourse of motherhood four months after becoming mothers felt significant guilt a year later when they were back at work. She explains that mothers who believe they must be home with their children rather than work outside the home tend to experience more guilt than those mothers who do not believe in that aspect of the discourse.

Mothers are exhausted not only because of what they have to do for their children but also because of the stress that is generated by the demands of the discourse. Let's use a typical internal monologue when caring for an infant to illustrate this argument. The baby needs to be fed, changed, and cuddled. At first glance, this seems like a simple task. But the reality is that babies cry, won't fall asleep, or they may wake up many times during the night. A task that on paper seems straightforward often triggers dissonance for mothers. They may experience self-doubt when the baby is not soothed even when his needs are met. So when the baby keeps crying, you want to go back to sleep but you ask yourself if it is harmful for the baby to cry without you being there. So you decide to bring the baby to your bed. Then you wonder if this is "healthy" for the baby or your marriage. You can certainly find support for your choice in the area of Attachment Parenting promoted by Dr. Sears (2001). He talks about the importance of the "family bed." Now you feel better about your choice. But the psychological stress does not end there. When your mother finds out, she tells you that having the baby sleep with you is terrible and that you are going to spoil the child and your marriage. The baby keeps waking up at night and you wonder if having him in your bed will prevent him from learning how to fall asleep by himself. You also wonder if he will become dependent on you rather than independent. Some friends tell you that you are going to turn him into a mama's boy and that he should learn to be independent. And what about your sex life? You sacrifice yourself because you think the baby is more important. If on the other hand, you decide to let the baby cry, you suffer and wonder if he will end up with attachment issues because you let him cry himself to sleep. Sound familiar? No wonder mothers are exhausted! We are not only doing the work of mothering but at every step we think that there is only one right path to take. And yet we do not have the guarantee that the choice we make is the right one, so we end up second guessing our decisions, and ourselves, often feeling inadequate, worried about the impact we will have on our children, and feeling guilty.

Guilt and feelings of inadequacy in mothers are not an intrinsic aspect of being a mother. They are a result of the dominant discourse of motherhood and about the position that mothers hold in society (Eyer, 1996). Diane Eyer, who wrote the book *Motherguilt: How our Culture Blames Mothers for What is Wrong with Society* examined the popular and empirical literature that burdens mothers with blame, and therefore feelings of guilt (1996). Eyer describes the burden on women who work outside of the home and who are also responsible for most of the child care and housework. This type of arrangement is creating unprecedented degrees of stress for mothers who often feel they are not doing either job well, which inevitably leads to those feelings of exhaustion, guilt, and inadequacy. Eyer also suggested that women's paid work is exploitative because women make much less than their male counterparts. Eyer stresses that women continue to be devalued and unsupported as mothers and that single mothers often are not in an economic position to take care of their children and find themselves feeling like bad mothers because they frequently need to be away from home to work.

Depression

An interesting fact is that women outnumber men in the incidence of depression. After childhood, more females than males report depression. Many psychologists have suggested that this is due at least in part to societal oppression and the ideologies of the perfect woman, perfect mother, and perfect beauty among others (Mauthner, 1999, 2010; Nicolson, 1998; Stoppard, 2000). Most women perceive themselves as falling short of these ideals and live with feelings of low self-worth. Furthermore, constantly aiming to meet these ideals limits their freedom and sense of well-being. Psychologists like Natasha Mauthner and Janet Stoppard argue that women today experience so much depression because they live under the oppression of these ideals. They argue against the medical model that implies that women experience depression due solely to biological factors. Stoppard and Mauthner suggest that depression in new mothers relates to experiences of loss, a lack of supportive, accepting, and non-judgmental interpersonal relationships, and to cultural contexts of historically specific, socially prescribed maternal practices.

Janet Stoppard, in her book *Understanding Depression: Feminist Social Constructionist Perspectives*, suggests that women are burdened by the beliefs of intensive mothering (2000). For example, she explains that a woman often will strive to engage in the practices of the good mother and interpret her chronic physical and emotional fatigue as part of the price of being a mother. She puts forth the idea that women who are unable to meet the demands set forth by the myths are more likely to experience stress, guilt, and possibly depression. Stoppard argues that what mothers experience as depression may be related to the distress, limitations, and a self-concept that are a result of their beliefs about mothering and what a good mother must be. Stoppard's work supports the contention that the beliefs about motherhood mask the deeper socio-cultural issues present in the lives of mothers.

Natasha Mauthner (1999, 2010) has conducted research on mothers who experienced post-partum depression. She found that this group experienced conflict between the mother they wanted to be and the mother they experienced themselves to be. This discrepancy increased their struggle to be good mothers. Each of these mothers experienced a different set of conflicts reflecting her own notion and belief of the "good mother" in regards to issues such as breastfeeding correctly, or having a drug free delivery. Mauthner explained the discrepancy in their experiences as deriving from two sources: the cultural pull due to norms and values surrounding motherhood and their actual, concrete, everyday experiences. During depressive episodes, these women found it difficult to let go of their images and ideals of motherhood so they tried to live up to them to avoid being labeled bad mothers. Mauthner found that the impact of the cultural pressures to be good mothers was mediated by their interpersonal lives. In other words, if their relationships supported and promoted the cultural myths, mothers were more likely to feel depressed. Moreover, negative spousal relationships made them feel inadequate because the lack of support left them alone in their attempt to "do it all" for their babies.

In sum, Stoppard and Mauthner argue that mothers' experiences of depression are not always biologically based but that by experiencing the pressures, responsibility, and blame that accompany their beliefs about motherhood, mothers call upon the label of depression to describe their experiences. Therefore, one can assume that the high expectations of the discourse are so powerful that they may compromise the mental health of many women.

Balancing employment and child care

Mothers are also faced with the question of whether they should work outside of the home. But this too can be a no-win situation. Mothers who stay home may experience societal judgment because they are not "working"; mothers who are employed may experience judgment because that they don't spend enough time with their children (Hays, 1996). Many mothers, in fact, do not have as an option to stay home. Other mothers do not work outside the home because they are told it is what is best for their children despite their own desire to work. And even those mothers who can and want to stay home experience being labeled "just a stay-at-home mom," which undervalues their labour and worth. The contradictory messages of needing to be at home *and* have a career can lead to feelings of inadequacy because the inherent impossibility of the opposing roles (Hays, 1996).

Other studies have investigated the pressures that mothers experience as they relate to paid employment and being mothers. Gillian Ranson, a sociologist at the University of Calgary, researched how some mothers make efforts to maintain identities as full-time mothers (1999). In her study, she included mothers who worked full-time, part-time, and who were home-based. All of the women held the belief that the best care for children should be done exclusively by the mother. These mothers made great efforts to balance paid employment and time with their children. They felt compelled to live by the full-time mother ideal even when they worked outside of the home. What this suggests is that many women buy into the belief that the best mother is the one who spends most of her time with her children. Ranson found that these mothers were rarely able to live up to the standard of the full-time mother because even those mothers who were home full-time, did not spend all of their time caring for, or attending to, their children. In other words, mothers who stay home do not spend all of their time with their children, but being a stay at home mom helped them feel like good mothers.

In addition, Ranson reported that for these mothers, other activities or housework were organized around the needs of their children. She suggests that some mothers are forced to live within these contradictions when they want to be identified as full-time mothers even when their lived experiences speak to the contrary. Ranson's study makes an important contribution by providing evidence that many mothers aspire to live up to the ideal of the stay-at-home mother. Regardless of their employment status, the women in her study felt that they must aspire to be with their children all the time and to schedule their lives around them. They only differed in how much flexibility they had in terms of being able to be home and in how balanced they felt their lives were in terms of pursuing employment/career versus raising their children. These women felt that they were obligated to provide their exclusive love and attention to their children at all times.

Sharon Hays also explored the contradictions of motherhood present in two opposing sets of expectations: the ideal of the good mother and the ideal of self-interested gain (employment) (1996). In order to examine the bases for these contradictions, Hays drew on three sources of data. She analyzed the history of childrearing, conducted an analysis of the best-selling contemporary child-rearing manuals, and interviewed 38 mothers of children between the ages of two and four. Hays found that both working and stay-at-home mothers shared a strong commitment to the ideology of intensive mothering. Similarly to Ranson's study (1999), they experienced the pushes and pulls of a no-win situation. If a mother stayed home with her children in order to live up to the ideal, she felt she was treated as an outcast. If a mother pursued paid employment, she paid the price of a double burden when she returned home to fulfill the demands of the mothering ideal. In both cases, mothers were pressured "to maintain the logic of intensive mothering" (p. 149). Hays explained that the complex strategies these mothers developed to manage the contradictions in their lives emphasized the emotional, cognitive, and physical consequences they experienced. Hays found that these women experienced strain because they were constantly making efforts to live by the ideology of intensive mothering. Her findings are another example of how the reality to live by the ideal of mothering is negatively impacting mothers.

Constant Anguish

Although there are many aspects of mothering that can be very rewarding, mothering has a dark side: anxiety, sleepless nights, an inability to soothe a baby, a lack of freedom to participate in self care, the frustration that accompanies an inability to control everything that impacts a child's development, loss of identity, anger felt towards children, lack of support between mothers, fear of making mistakes and then "ruining" a child, ongoing judgment, and having the option to make desired choices to meet the expectations of the ideal mother. Judith Warner addresses these shortfalls in her book *Perfect Madness* when she writes,

> Many, many others would like to stay home with their children and can't afford to do so. Many others would like to be able to maintain their full-time careers without either being devoured or losing ground, and they can't do that. Many can't work without experiencing agonies of guilt because the quality of child care their salaries can provide for is so low. Many can't stay home without losing their minds because child care is so expensive they can't afford to get a break. (2006, p. 265)

Wanting to do it right, and realizing daily that it is impossible, can cause great stress for mothers, who then worry about how their children might turn out. Judith Warner writes:

> ... [there is] a feeling. That caught-by-the-throat feeling so many mothers have today of always doing something wrong ... [it is] lowering our horizons and limiting our minds. Sapping energy that we should have for our children and ourselves. And drowning our thoughts that might lead us, collectively, to formulate solutions. The feeling has many faces, but it doesn't really have a name. It's not depression. It's not oppression. It's a mix of things, a kind of *too muchness*. An existential discomfort. A mess. (2006, back cover)

Whichever way we call it, the feeling is intense. Many mothers believe it goes with the territory and there is nothing to be done, and they must therefore put up with these feelings. Judith Warner (2006) interviewed dozens of mothers and she found that when mothers spoke about their anxiety regarding abandonment and the now-famous separation anxiety, they spoke more about their own feelings than their children's. Mothers' fears can be well out of proportion with the real dangers that children face today. For example, they fear that children are in serious danger if they play outside without supervision. However, there is no evidence to suggest, for example, that there are more child kidnappings than there were 50 or 60 years ago (Glassner, 1999).

The unprecedented levels of anxiety and anguish that mothers experience are a consequence of our need to perform, suggests Judith Warner. She argues that the anguish we experience is related to the fact that we live in an era where competitiveness, individuality, isolation, perfectionism, independence, achievement, status, power, and the generation of money are of extreme importance. In sum, many women are not always enjoying being mothers; they live in fear of making mistakes rather feeling empowered to carve out their own path.

Silence and Isolation

In addition to experiencing the negative aspects of motherhood, mothers are expected to maintain a code of silence. Susan Maushart, in her book *The Mask of Motherhood,* writes about the "fronts" that mothers put out to the world while hiding the reality of their experience (2000). She calls this the mask of motherhood. She explains that these fronts involve having a mask that conveys courage, serenity, and being all-knowing; yet behind the mask mothers feel angry, frustrated, tired, confused, and exhausted. According to Maushart, it is the mask of motherhood that keeps women silent about their true feelings and suspicious about what they know. This mask is what minimizes the extent of women's work in the world. It is having to wear this mask that forces mothers not to talk to others about feeling angry at their child or wanting to run and hide sometimes. It is this expectation of silence that prevents mothers from saying that they don't always feel loving toward their children when they are acting out, or that mothering can be exhausting and frustrating.

I remember when my girls were five and one and I had a terrible cold. I had a headache that was splitting my head in two, I was so congested that I couldn't breathe, and I needed to sleep! My one year old was playing and hanging around in her diaper and I knew I had to watch her but I couldn't stay awake. I didn't have anyone to help. So I lay on the sofa and literally kept one eye open and one closed. It was so painful to not be able to just be sick and sleep. I had no one to be angry at, but I hated the experience. I am not suggesting that I hated my daughter, but there were many occasions that were frustrating and I was not allowed to complain. I had to pretend motherhood was wonderful all the time when, in fact, I had many experiences that I found horrible. This type of silence is very harmful to mothers because we cannot access each other for support. More importantly, we feel isolated and bad because we don't hear about anyone else feeling these negative emotions, we feel guilty because we are unable to be happy all the time like all the other mothers we see at the park.

When women plan to have children, they often imagine it is going to be a fairy tale. They think of a sweet bundle of joy that will make them happy and fulfilled and bring them closer to their partner. In short, they imagine bliss. I was teaching a class recently at the University of British Columbia on family education and consultation. The topic for that particular day was motherhood. I asked the students why so many people want to have children when they've never experienced it. In the same vein, how can someone desperately crave chocolate ice cream if they have never tried it? One student said, "You would if everyone told you that it was so delicious and so great that you would want to experience it!" "Exactly!" I said. That is the point. Social messaging tells us that being a parent is an amazing, rewarding, and loving experience and that everyone ought to try it. I agree that being a mother is amazing, rewarding, and full of lessons; I have loved being a mom. I have learned many things about love, human nature, growth, relationships, commitment, values, courage, myself, and anger, sadness, worry, and terror. It is these darker aspects of motherhood (anger, sadness, worry, and terror) that no one talks about.

So being a mother can be laden with sorrow, anger, frustration, fatigue, guilt, and confusion. These feelings manifest themselves early in the lives of mothers. Many of these emotions are derived simply from loving our children and wanting the best for them; others are a result of the challenges that come with assuming the responsibility for another human being; yet others are directly connected to the dominant discourse of motherhood. Maushart (2000) explains that having children changes mothers significantly and in irreversible ways but that if a mother is to admit this publicly it would be like publishing that Santa Claus does not exist. She explains that the mask of motherhood is the external and obvious sign of this silent conspiracy. It is the open face of motherhood that hides from others and from ourselves the centrality of our common mission. We may not be able to avoid some of the things that happen to cause us grief—such as our child becoming sick, not sleeping at night, needing to be kept safe and alive, experiencing unfortunate events, and so on—but we can certainly resist the oppression of the dominant discourse of motherhood. We can redefine our roles as well as our perceptions of what a mother is and we can team up with the rest of the mother population in a sisterhood of sorts rather than being our own worst enemies.

This last point is crucial to our realities as mothers. "The look." We all know it. That look that mothers give one another in disapproval. We are all so quick to judge. We act as though we know the right answers, as if our beliefs were the only right ones. This judgment takes many forms: a stay-at-home mother's judgment over another who takes her child to daycare full-time; a working mother's judgment over another who stays home and does not "pursue a career"; one mother's judgment at the playground over another whose child is "misbehaving" or not getting along with other children. In these ways, we enforce the dominant discourse on ourselves. We perpetuate the discourse so that it might be alive long enough to oppress our own daughters. We can contribute to changing the dominant discourse by changing the way we treat one another. Mothers must honour and respect each other. We must realize that most mothers love their children and do the best they can. We must support each other in our differences.

To summarize, it is apparent that the dominant discourse of motherhood impacts the lives of mothers in many ways. Many mothers experience guilt and depression. They strain to maintain a close physical presence with their children and to maintain their status as full-time mothers. They feel pressured to live by the dominant discourse of motherhood, which promotes a set of beliefs about how to be a good mother but that are not based on fact. This discourse, as discussed in this chapter, is harmful to mothers because it robs mothers of freedom, peace, confidence, balance, self-esteem, time, and trust. As Andrea O'Reilly suggests, the dominant discourse of motherhood robs mothers of agency, authority, and autonomy (O'Reilly, 2004).

Given all this and that the current dominant discourse of motherhood is so oppressive to women, it is time to explore alternative ways of mothering that can allow women to experience motherhood in a more agented, empowered, and autonomous way. The reality of not being able to live up to the ideal of the perfect mother has pushed many women to reconsider how they are mothering their children and to make choices that work best for them. The following chapter introduces the women who shared their stories of resistance with me and presents the many ways in which they resisted the dominant discourse.

Chapter 3

The Many Faces of Resistance

To seek visions, to dream dreams, is essential to try new ways of living, to make room for serious experimentation, to respect the effort even where it fails.
—Adrienne Rich, *Of Woman Born*

THE LITERATURE ON MOTHERHOOD AND MOTHERING in the latter part of the twentieth century has focused on the oppressive dominant discourse of motherhood and how it is destructive toward women (Hays, 1996; Rich, 1986; Thurer, 1994). A multitude of scholarly books and articles fought to raise women's awareness about this phenomenon. Adrian Rich exposed the realities of motherhood and how the patriarchal discourse of motherhood is oppressive to women. Sharon Hays wrote about the contradictions of motherhood and coined the term "intensive mothering" in an attempt to describe the current practices of motherhood. Shari Thurer wrote about the history of motherhood, exposing the factors that influenced our current dominant discourse of motherhood. This literature highlights the problem but it fails to explore how many mothers struggle to resist their oppression. Furthermore, by only writing about the dominant discourse and how it affects women, these writers painted women as passive victims of the discourse. Although some of these scholars emphasized the importance of resistance (Rich, 1986), no one has explored whether women were indeed resisting or has described their lived experience of resistance. Although at the time I conducted my study Tula Gordon (1990) had performed a study on feminist mothers who were resisting the discourse, her study only included women who identified as feminist, which excluded many other mothers. This gap in the literature was problematic because it prevents us from having the larger picture about mothers who resist. It is now time to expand our discussion and understanding to include women who are actively resisting and exploring alternative ways to mother.

In this chapter, I discuss how fifteen mothers redefined mothering in a process of resistance to the dominant discourse of motherhood. These women resisted in a manner that, although challenging at times, was empowering to them. This suggests that women can be responsible, caring mothers and feel close to their children while resisting the dominant discourse of motherhood. By developing what is called a critical consciousness, mothers can begin to develop a more positive identity as mothers and to let go of the social pressures and myths that are unhelpful and, at times, harmful.

Resistance in this context refers to the act of joining other mothers in fighting against beliefs that oppress mothers generally. It means listening to our own intuition and trusting ourselves rather than always having to consult the advice of "experts." It means honouring ourselves as much as our children. It means not being a slave to our children and instead involving them in running the home. It means finding an identity as a human being and not only as a "good mother." It means anything that leads mothers to have a higher quality of life during the years that they are actively mothering. It means acknowledging that children matter, but so do mothers.

What is Resistance?

Many publications that offer a critique of the institution of motherhood portray mothers as passive victims who may have no recourse against such a powerful force. However, human beings have historically resisted societal oppression and mothers are no exception. For the purposes of my study, resistance was defined as the effort of oppressed groups to challenge and act against aspects of dominant discourses (Scott, 1990). In other words, resistance here refers to the effort of mothers to challenge and act against aspects of the dominant discourse of motherhood.

The women I interviewed perceived themselves as resistant to this discourse. They volunteered to share their stories and describe not only how they resisted, but also how resistance impacted their mothering experiences. I suspect that a large number of mothers resist—according to my definition—even when they don't name their actions as resistance. Given that the expectations of the dominant discourse are impossible to achieve, I suppose that many women are resisting and being creative in how they mother. However, many mothers feel guilty and still hope to achieve the ideal. Resistance is a *conscious* process that is based on being actively involved in critical evaluation of the societal expectations on mothers and the discourses of childhood, womanhood, and family. With awareness of the impossibility of the ideal, and how some of the expectations on mothers are unrealistic and not beneficial to mothers or their children, mothers can consciously resist. It is this consciousness that leads to an experience of empowerment; by making choices that are guided by this awareness, mothers can rise above guilt and feelings of deficiency, and change their lives.

The Women in the Study

I provide below an introductory description of the fifteen women that I interviewed and whose names have been replaced by pseudonyms to protect their identities. I hope that when you read their stories throughout the book, you suspend judgment; these are mothers who love and care about their children, regardless of how they mother. Furthermore, I hope that as you read these pages, you engage in this exercise with a willingness to embrace all mothers who care about their children and who choose the best way to mother from their own perspective.

All of the mothers lived in the Metro Vancouver area in British Columbia, Canada, volunteered to be interviewed, and gave consent for their stories to be told. The interviews occurred over two days and on average I spent between two and three hours talking with them. The women told me about their lives in their own fashion. Although I had a series of questions prepared, they could add or highlight issues or topics they felt were important. I analyzed their narratives from verbatim transcripts of the interviews (see Horwitz, 2003, for a detailed description of the interview questions and analysis).

The women's ages ranged from 23 to 46 years old. Their income levels ranged between CAD$15,000 and over CAD$75,000 a year. Their educational levels varied from one year of college to current Ph.D. candidacy. Three worked full-time, seven worked and/or went to school part-time, and five were stay-at-home mothers. All but three were in heterosexual relationships, two were single, and one was gay and single. They were all white. I have struggled to classify some of them into middle- or low-income class. Although all of them had some post-secondary education, which could be considered middle class, three were in an income bracket that is considered to be low. Four had relinquished the role of main caregiver to their partners and were the main breadwinners for their families. Refer to Appendix A for a detailed summary of the participants' background information. I will now introduce the 15 participants.

Louise

Louise was 46-years old and had two daughters who were nine and 14 at the time of our interview. Louise had been married for 21 years and was enrolled in a master's degree program. Her annual family income was in the range of CAD$61,000 to CAD$75,000. She spent most of her adult life participating in competitive sports even while having young children. She resisted the dominant discourse of motherhood because she did not believe that she needed to be around her children all the time or that mothers are the only ones who can care for and guide children. She believed that others can contribute to their development. Louise made time to pursue her athletic career, which meant she was away from her children on occasion. Finally, Louise did not feel solely responsible for how her children turn out; she recognized that there are other factors that impact their development.

Anna

Anna was a 39-year-old mother of two, a twelve-year-old girl and a ten-year-old boy. She had been married for 16 years and worked as a professional in a college setting. Anna had just finished a master's degree when we met. Her annual family income was in the range of CAD$46,000 to CAD$60,000. Anna felt that she resisted the discourse because she did not feel that she had to be with her children all the time; she liked involving other caregivers so that she could pursue her career. Anna believed that mothers are not the only ones who can nurture children and did not find motherhood completely fulfilling. She explained that she needed other experiences in her life to feel fulfilled. Finally, Anna did not believe that she is to blame for all of her children's behaviors or how they turn out. Anna explained that she had learned that each mother and her children are unique and this has led her to make unique choices that work for her family. Anna did not like being a full-time mother and was aware that she had been able to make the choices she has made because of her position in society and because of the historical times within which she was mothering.

Carla

Carla was a 27-year-old mother of a one-year-old girl. She was in a heterosexual common-law relationship of four years. She was a full-time student enrolled in a Ph.D. program. Her family's annual income was in the range of CAD$46,000 to CAD$60,000. Carla identified herself as resistant because she relinquished the main caregiving role to her partner. She was caring and involved but did not mind being away from the baby when her husband or in-laws cared for her. Carla did not feel solely responsible for how her daughter was going to turn out. Finally, Carla strived to meet her own needs and interests while also meeting those of her daughter.

Astrid

Astrid was a 30-year-old mother of a three-year-old boy and an eight month-old girl. She had been married for eight years. Her family income was in the range of CAD$31,000 to CAD$45,000. Astrid was a not employed outside of the home. She was an artist whose art, she said, was not commercial or sellable. Astrid was involved in La Leche League as a group leader, was a parent group leader, and was an active participant at her son's preschool.

Astrid clarified that all these activities were volunteer endeavors but she questioned others that say that she "did not work." Astrid resisted by not following the dictates of the mainstream medical model of childrearing; she practiced extended breastfeeding, for example. She also resisted individualistic parenting strategies that suggest that children need to be independent and sleep in their own beds, and separate psychologically from their parents at an early age. She practices Attachment Parenting. She resisted the idea that mothers should sacrifice their needs but found that the only way mothers can avoid sacrificing is by having a closely-knit community of supportive and emotionally invested people, which she lacked. Astrid defined herself as a feminist who honours not only her own needs but also those of her children. She believed that mothers should not be the only ones to care for children but that in individualistic societies, women are isolated and therefore, the only ones "mothering" children.

Aibrean

Aibrean was a 26-year-old mother of a seven year-old boy and a five month-old girl. She had her son when she was 19 and single. She was a single mother for three-and-a-half years, when she met her present husband. She had been married for one-and-a-half years at the time of our interviews. Aibrean was not employed outside of the home. Her annual family income was in the range of CAD$15,000 to CAD$30,000. Aibrean resisted because she did not believe in sacrificing her needs; she would attend to things that mattered to her even if it meant not washing the dishes or cleaning the house. She was willing to let her baby cry for short periods while she painted her nails or practiced self-care because she did not think this would harm the baby. She did not take sole responsibility for how her children behaved. She believed that there are other factors—such as biology or school—that affect who her children are and who they become. Finally, Aibrean explained that she voices to others that she does not like being a mother all the time, and that even though she loves her children, she does not "feel loving" toward them all the time. She had encountered judgment for saying this, but believes it is important to recognize and voice it.

Theo

Theo was a 30-year-old mother of a 21-month-old girl. She had been with her husband for 10 years. Theo was a doula, group facilitator, and student. Her annual family income was in the range of CAD$46,000 to CAD$60,000. Theo indicated that she was convinced of the choices that she makes relating to her daughter. Theo resisted because she believed that mothers need to acknowledge the hardships that come with being a mother. She made it a point to speak out about the 'dark' side of mothering infants and how a mother can experience anger toward her children. She resisted the mainstream medical model by giving birth at home and practising extended breast-feeding. She also believed that mothers have a right to pursue their interests and did not find mothering fulfilling on its own. At the same time, she found that because her child was very young, it was very difficult to balance her child's needs and her own. Theo did not see herself as being responsible for all of her child's behaviors. Finally, Theo believed that it was very important to involve others in raising children and that being close to many others exposes a child to different experiences and more affection. Theo disliked that people expected her to feel a certain way in relation to mothering because her actual experience was very different. She explained that she did not always feel happy to be a mother or loving toward her child.

Alice

Alice was a 31-year-old mother of two boys who were seven and three years-old. She had been married for eight years. Alice was not employed outside of the home, but she was a fiction writer who worked late at night or when her husband took the children out. Alice began writing again when she realized that motherhood had become too absorbing for her. Her annual family income was over CAD$75,000. Alice resisted because she recognized that mothering was not completely fulfilling for her. She loved her children but needed to pursue other interests. Alice resisted the mainstream medical model; she gave birth to her sons at home and chose not to vaccinate them. Alice did not believe that there is only one way to mother. She resisted the "new ideal" that is encouraged by "Hollywood mothers like Madonna and Demi Moore" who promote the belief that "mothers can do it all, be thin, beautiful, and dedicated." Finally, Alice questioned the societal myth that suggests that children are innocent and should be sheltered from what is real. She believed in open discussions about any topic with her sons.

Madelaine

Madelaine was a 36-year-old woman of two boys who were six and ten years old. She had been married for 13 years. Madelaine was a writer and editor who was working 30 hours a week. Up to one year before we met, she did most of her work at home. At the time of our interviews, Madelaine was going to the office two days a week and working the rest of the time at home. Her family's annual income was over CAD$75,000. Madelaine explained that she resisted the myths of mothering because she did not follow the mainstream medical model of parenting. She chose not to vaccinate her children and practiced extended breast-feeding. In addition, she resisted individualistic strategies of parenting children and practiced Attachment Parenting. Madelaine did not find mothering fulfilling on its own; she always needed to pursue other interests such as writing or yoga. She did not believe that the mother should carry out all the caregiving of children alone, but in her circumstances, she had had to take on that role because when she first became a mother she had few resources to carry out alternative practices. Madelaine believed that she had a right to mother her own way rather than following the dictates of the dominant discourse of motherhood. Finally, Madelaine had been a political activist and participated in activism to establish recognition of the fact that the work mothers do is work.

Lilith

Lilith was a 23-year-old mother of two girls who were toddlers. She was a single mother and a full-time undergraduate student. Her annual family income was in the range of CAD$15,000 to CAD$30,000. Up until two years before we met, Lilith had a Grade 10 education. By the time we met she had completed her high school equivalency and started a degree in the social sciences. She was living alone with her daughters. Lilith felt that she resisted the discourse because she did not believe she should be with her daughters during all of her free time. Even though she was busy with her university studies, she went out most weekends with friends or dates. She was very active in political issues that affect her and other mothers. Lilith questioned most of what was expected of her and rebelled against the status quo. She did not feel guilty for having fun or for taking a smoking break outside on her front porch and away from her children. She did not believe that mothers are the only possible caregivers of children; she believed that daycare providers could contribute significantly. She did not follow the medical model; for example, she did not vaccinate her daughters. Lilith did not view her role as a mother to be a perfect housekeeper who should clean and cook constantly.

Jane

Jane was a 37-year-old mother of a three year-old girl and a seven month-old boy. She had been married for six years. Jane had been a health worker in the past and was currently teaching at a college while completing a graduate degree. A year before the interview, Jane's family was struggling financially. She explained how painful it was not to have money to buy small Christmas gifts for her children. Since then, Jane had found a job that paid "well." Her annual family income varied but at the time of the interview it was in the range of CAD$61,000 to CAD$75,000. Jane resisted the societal expectations on mothers because she believed that she had a right to take care of her needs and pursue her interests. She had relinquished the primary caregiving role to her husband who had taken most of the parental leave to stay home with the children while she pursued her graduate degree and worked outside of the home. Jane did not believe in remaining in the private sphere; she was an activist. She considered fathers to be as good as mothers in caring for children. She did not believe that she was solely responsible for how her children turned out and explained that there were other factors involved. She resisted the medical model of birth and care and was active in promoting the benefits of extended breastfeeding.

Jane explained that she did not pay attention to the dominant discourse of motherhood most of the time because she endeavored to do what was best for her. She said that making her own choices had eliminated her experience of guilt for the most part. Jane saw her role as having to set the structure for her children but not to have to "micromanage" by always being near. She believed that it was important for children to be close to many adults, not only their mothers. Finally, for Jane it was very important that her professional and activism work contribute to the welfare of mothers in general.

Catherine

Catherine was a 33-year-old mother of a seven year-old girl. She had been married for 12 years. She had worked full-time outside of the home in a professional occupation until recently when she had arranged for two days each week to be worked from home. Her annual family income was CAD$75,000 or more. Catherine shared that she resisted the dominant discourse of motherhood because she had relinquished the primary caregiving role to her husband. Because he was able to work from home, they decided that he should be the one to take on the role of primary caregiver. Catherine saw him as the better parent, and was happy with her choice to not take on the primary role. She, therefore, did not believe that mothers should always be the main caregivers of children. Moreover, Catherine believed that her needs and her relationship should be nurtured so that they as a couple could then nurture their child. She was not completely fulfilled by her role as a mother. Finally, she did not believe that mothers should "do it all."

Alexandra

Alexandra was a 41-year-old mother of an eight year-old girl. She had been married for nine years at the time of our interview. Her family annual income was more than CAD$75,000. Alexandra works in a professional occupation that is very demanding. She resisted the dominant discourse of motherhood because she had relinquished the primary caregiving role to her husband whose work allowed him to stay home. Alexandra was very involved in her daughter's life but did not view herself as her daughter's main caregiver. Alexandra did not believe in sacrificing her needs for her daughter; she sometimes placed her needs ahead of her daughter's.

Finally, Alexandra explained that she did not always want to spend time with her daughter.

Nancy

Nancy was a 46-year-old mother of three children, a 16 year-old girl and two boys, twelve and eight years-old. Nancy had been married for 20 years. She was a professional who worked part-time during evenings and school hours. She enjoyed athletics. Her annual family income was above CAD$75,000. Nancy resisted the dominant discourse of motherhood because she believed in voicing and recognizing that mothering can have negative aspects and is not always enjoyable. She believed that it is fine to sleep in the same bed with children when they are young. She was convinced that mothers have a right to take care of their needs and sometimes to put these ahead of their children's as long as it is safe for the children and not neglectful. Nancy did not see herself as solely responsible for how her children 'turn out'. She believed that she and her partner were co-parents who share the responsibility for their children. Finally, Nancy did not find motherhood to be fulfilling on its own; she needed to be involved in other interests.

Kate

Kate was a 36-year-old mother of two boys who were four and six years old at the time of the interview. She had been married for 12 years. She worked 20 hours a week as a fundraiser. Her annual family income was in the range of CAD$61,000 to CAD$75,000. Kate resisted because she did not believe in having to watch her children at all times. She thought that the media has "overblown" the dangers for children. She believed in participating in a community that supports each other in raising children: she lived in a family co-op where children played unsupervised in closed courtyards and other parents were always available in case of an emergency. Kate did not believe that mothers are the only ones who can influence and care for children. She believed that children are safe if left at daycare or with other caregivers and she did not feel guilty about doing so herself. She did not think that mothers should cater to children but rather that children should cooperate with the running of a home; she made sure her sons participated in the functioning of their home. Kate did not feel solely responsible for how her children turn out. She considered that mothers should voice their frustrations and that they do not always like being mothers. Finally, Kate believed that her needs were important; she sometimes placed them ahead of her children's but often tried to achieve a "win-win" situation where both parties have their needs met. Kate emphasized that she did not believe in taking responsibility or credit for how her children behave. She explained that her children's personalities are 'easy' and that this contributed to her performance as a good mother.

Lisa

Lisa was a 33-year-old, single mother of a four year-old girl. Lisa had recently separated from her husband of eight years. Part of the reason for this separation is that she had recently come out as a gay woman. Her family's annual income was in the range of CAD$15,000 to CAD$30,000. Lisa felt she resisted the myths of mothering because she was co-parenting with her daughter's father and did not consider herself the only caregiver for her daughter. She did not believe that mothers should do it all by themselves. She did not believe in having to choose between spending time with her child and being involved in other activities that are of interest to her. She often felt guilty about having dissolved her marriage and about not being domestic enough to teach her daughter about those aspects of life.

The Many Faces of Resistance

Resistance never looks exactly the same. The purpose of this book is not to promote specific instructions on how or what to resist, but rather to show that women are resisting and that this process is experienced as empowering regardless of how she resists. The women who I interviewed resisted in a variety of ways. Sometimes their resistance was not manifested in their practices but in their ideologies and perception of themselves. The number and types of aspects of the dominant discourse of motherhood that each participant resisted varied significantly. Moreover, not only the degree and quality of resistance varied, but also the extent to which they struggled to resist. Some found resistance to be a relatively smooth process while others found it challenging and difficult. The analysis of the interviews yielded the following modes of resistance:

1. Resistance by making myself count
   a. Resisting by meeting my needs and/or pursuing my interests is important.
   b. Deriving fulfillment not only from mothering but also from other things in my life.
   c. Not being around my children all the time.

2. Resistance by involving others
   a. Involving partners as primary caregivers.
   b. Practicing co-parenting.
   c. Involving others/community.
   d. Not doing it all.

3. Resistance by actively questioning and/or actively voicing views
   a. Actively questioning expectations.
   b. Voicing views/experience.

4. Resistance by questioning mainstream medicine/ individualistic approaches to child-rearing
   a. Resisting the mainstream medical model.
   b. Practicing child focused and/or attachment parenting.

5. Resistance that involves the role of mother
   a. Not being responsible for all of my children's behaviours or how they turn out.
   b. Not feeling loving toward my children all the time.
   c. Not cooking and/or cleaning as my main role.
   d. Not taking credit or blame.

What follows is a closer examination of these different ways in which the women I interviewed resisted.

Resistance by Making Myself Count

Resisting by meeting my needs and/or pursuing my interests is important. All the women in this study expressed that it is important for them to meet their own needs or pursue their own interests. Their interests included athletics, graduate school, writing, taking time out, work, exercise, mundane activities, and so on. The degree to which they were able to meet their needs or pursue their interests varied. For example, Carla, Jane, Catherine, and Alexandra's partners were the primary caregivers of their children, which freed them to pursue their careers and take time for other activities such as reading and exercise. Catherine said, "I think that in order to be whole, you have to be healthy and happy and take care of yourself physically, and mentally, emotionally, before you can give to your spouse. And then as a couple you give to your children." Others like Louise, Anna, Lilith, and Kate found community in friends, family, daycare, and baby-sitting co-ops and this allowed them to pursue their careers or take some time for themselves. Some of the women explained that they believed in meeting their needs and pursuing their interests but that they found it difficult because they lacked the social supports to do so. Astrid, for example, explained that she had a right to her interests but that she does not have any family nearby and it is difficult to find someone to provide child care to her children. Finally, Lisa expressed that she is interested in other endeavours including "challenging conversation" or art exhibits but that she is often unable to pursue those because society does not allow mothers to include their children in these types of activity. Whether they were able to fulfill their needs or not, all the women expressed having a right to do so.

Deriving fulfillment not only from mothering but also from other things in my life. "Yeah, and I know I am not completely fulfilled by the mothering role," said Jane. As her comment connotes, mothers whose resistance fell into this category expressed that, even though mothering is important to them, they also need other experiences to feel fulfilled. For example, Catherine and Alexandra explained that there is no one thing in their lives that is fulfilling on its own; they need variety to feel satisfied. Catherine said, "I do not think that any one thing in life makes you whole." Others found that their initial experiences as mothers were difficult, which led them to seek other activities to feel fulfilled. For example, Anna explained that motherhood, particularly in the early stages, did not allow her to feel competent because her baby was a very difficult infant who cried constantly. For her, mothering during that period did not fulfill her needs so she sought involvement in her work to feel competent: "If I was going to love that baby, have any quality time with that baby, I have to get away from that baby. I have to meet my own needs, and my own needs of being competent." Finally, Lisa, in contrast to the rest of the mothers, expressed that, because she is "child focused," she has found fulfillment in being a mother but does not expect that this will be the case after her child is five and therefore more independent. She expected to return to work at that time: "I mean, I'm going to go back to work next year. But, I think I'll really be able to focus on that more, because she's going to have her own space and her own time. But at the moment, when she's more dependent on me..." In conclusion, these women explicitly expressed that fulfillment for them is derived from a variety of experiences, not just from mothering.

Not being around my children all the time. These women expressed that they did not believe they had to be around their children all the time; they did not see that as necessary for their children's well-being or to be good mothers. Carla, for example, said, "I don't think you have to be with your child constantly for a strong bond to develop. I think as long as you're there frequently and as long as you are loving and consistent...there is going to be a strong bond." Jane stated, "I don't think that a mother has to be around 100 percent of the time to be a good mother." Alexandra and Catherine explained that they believe in being available for their daughters but not all the time. Alice, on the other hand, had chosen to be home with her children and has chosen to home-school her children. She explained that, as mothering took over and absorbed her, she realized this was becoming a problem so she began to pursue her writing career in order to keep a balance.

So I was focusing on mothering all the time. I had chosen it as an escape from life.... It's like before I had my kids I was the Richard Stein, with the cigar in the mouth and the F word. And suddenly I was this ultra-domesticated woman...I've got to find something to do or I am going to go out of my mind. So I went back to writing.

These women explained that motherhood couldn't fulfill them. They found that they needed to pursue other interests in order to "be happy" and "feel whole."

Resistance by Involving Others

Involving partners as primary caregivers. Four of the women's husbands were the primary caregivers of their children (Carla, Jane, Catherine, Alexandra). These women were pursuing careers and education while their husbands were at home taking care of their children. Jane and Carla's husbands took parental leave when their children were born. Carla went back to work two weeks after her baby was born; Jane went back after three months. Alexandra and Catherine shared taking care of their infant daughters with their partners for the first few months and then chose to return to work while their husbands took care of their children. Three of these women all expressed that this arrangement freed them to pursue their careers and interests without feeling guilty for leaving their children behind.

Practicing co-parenting. In addition to the women whose husbands were the primary caregivers of their children, some reported that their husbands were equal partners in parenting their children and also saw themselves as co-parents. These women emphasized that they shared the care of their children with their husbands. Lisa recently separated from her husband but he continued to share equally in the care of their daughter. Madelaine also expressed that she believed that partnership and co-parenting are desirable goals, but that because her husband was initially unable to participate equally due to illness and work difficulties, they developed "patterns of care" that placed her as the main caregiver. This resulted in her children seeing her as their main source of guidance and support. Finally, Lilith stood out as unique in this category because she was, and always had been, a single mother; she did not have a partner with whom to share responsibility. She involved several trusted friends and daycare providers in helping her raise her children.

Involving others/community. Most of the women had either involved others in helping them with their children, or believed in involving others but were unable to do so. These women thought that having access to a supportive community when raising children is essential. Louise explained that, because her partner traveled "off and on" for nine months of the year, she had had to seek a community for herself and her children: "I believe in community parenting!" For example, she participated in baby-sitting co-ops, asked family to help her, organized pot-luck dinners, and participated in athletic activities with and without her daughters. Astrid, on the other hand, had only recently moved to the Vancouver area and still felt quite isolated. Even though she made efforts to find supports, she found it very difficult to build a community for herself and her family.

It is important to note that all of the women but four did not believe in, or like, leaving their children in daycare centres. They did not want to pay for someone to care for their children. They believed that adults who help them should have love for, and an investment in the well being of, their children. These women emphasized that the way society is structured does not allow for a natural community experience that includes various loving adults collaborating in the upbringing of children. These women explained that this leads them to actively seek ways to create community for themselves and their children.

Kate emphasized that living within a community where the children could go out and play freely without needing parental supervision at all times was ideal for her. She lived in co-operative housing in Vancouver: "We lived in a co-op with enclosed courtyards. And it was really the best possible set up for little kids because, from a really early age, they would just go out the door. There were so many eyes on the courtyard, which was enclosed so it was fabulous. It was really a nice safe place." Kate explained that she experienced how community made her feel connected and supported. In addition to living in this setting for many years, she always felt comfortable leaving her children with baby sitters: "And from a very early age I left Ian with baby sitters, and always thought that that was a very healthy thing."

Not doing it all. Some mothers expressed that they did not believe they should have to do it all. Astrid explained that she believed in being with her children and seeing them develop but that she does not believe that she should have to do it all by herself; she would prefer to be part of a supportive community where people would share in supporting each other. Catherine did not believe that she should have to do it all herself so she chose a partner who shares equally in running the household and taking care of their child. Finally, Madelaine explained that she would have liked her partner to be more involved not only with the children but also with the running of the household. She believed that they developed strong patterns within which she does most of those tasks and that these patterns would now be difficult to change.

Resistance by Actively Questioning and/ or Actively Voicing Views

Actively questioning expectations. Several of the women expressed that they actively engage in questioning the expectations that are placed on them by others and society. All mothers in the study engaged in some sort of questioning at one time or another, but six of the women's stories revealed that questioning is central to how they experience mothering and resist the dominant discourse. Astrid found the experience of mothering so difficult at the beginning because her son would not stop crying that she began searching for ways to make sense of her experience. She read feminist literature and began to question the social forces that affected her experience: the lack of community for mothers who choose to stay home, the views that mothers who stay home are "doormats" and sacrificial, and so on. She did not view herself as a "doormat" and was not willing "to compromise [her] right to have close and connected relationships with [her] children."

Aibrean described herself as a "questioner" and Lilith as someone who always "questioned the status quo." Both of these women stated that they always asked questions about societal norms and expectations since their youth. They both stated that they have continued this practice with regards to mothering. Alice, Madelaine, and Lisa also appeared to question how society tells them they should mother. For example, they questioned accepted norms such as: boys and girls should be raised differently because of their gender, children do not belong at certain types of events, or children should attend school because it is good for them. Finally, several of them stated that they question the value of materialism, which led them to make efforts to raise their children in alternative ways. For example, Aibrean explained that she does not work because she believes in being home with her children, she would rather be home and have a limited amount of money than to go to work just to buy her children "things" at the expense of being around them. All these mothers explained that questioning often led to choices that are not "mainstream."

Voicing views/experience. These women stated that they voice their views or experience formally or informally. Astrid, Theo, Madelaine, Lilith, and Jane considered themselves activists for women and mothers. Astrid participated in groups for parents where she voiced her views about patriarchy and its impact on mothers, children, and families. Theo was a doula who believes in telling new or expecting parents about the difficulties of caring for an infant. Madelaine had been involved in a feminist organization where she did research and advocacy in support of the view that mothers' work is work. Lilith attended demonstrations and wrote to politicians to protest the treatment of single mothers in British Columbia. Jane was actively involved in supporting mothers who want to engage in extended breastfeeding.

Aibrean, Nancy, Kate, Theo, and Lilith all believed that mothers should be free to express the difficulties of being a mother. Nancy explained that sometimes she felt like she was going crazy and she hated her child. Being able to voice this to her friends was very helpful in maintaining her mental health. Kate, Aibrean, and Lilith told similar stories. They felt relieved when they shared their frustrations with others.

Resisting by Questioning Mainstream Medical/Individualistic Approaches to Child-Rearing

Resisting the mainstream medical model. Several of the women reported that some of their practices were not in agreement with the mainstream medical model on birthing, breastfeeding, and vaccinations. These women chose to practice extended breast-feeding, which means that they breastfed their children between one-and-a-half and four years. Astrid explained that breastfeeding enhances the bond between mother and child. Jane, who is an activist for extended breastfeeding said, "Actually the research shows that breastfeeding two years and beyond is a good thing for the child and for the mom, healthy for bonding, and a number of other reasons."

Aibrean, Theo, and Alice all chose to have home births. They explained that there are many women who do this but it is still uncommon. Aibrean said it was a good option for her: "I think it's the very best choice women can make." They found that many people including their families and friends were opposed to or critical of this choice. Theo explained that her mother-in-law was a nurse who was very vocal against home births. All three women explained that they researched the topic in depth and felt very confident that their decision was the right one for them and that home births are indeed safe.

Finally, Alice, Madelaine, and Lilith explained that they chose not to vaccinate their children. They performed extensive research that led them to make this choice. Alice explained that the decision was not easy but that after doing some research, she decided that this was the best thing for her children. These three women explained that they have been criticized for making this choice. Alice said, "As if I had not carefully decided, as if I had not really gone through, you know, difficulty as to what to do with them."

Practicing child focused and/or Attachment Parenting. A few of these mothers resisted the individualistic aspects of the dominant discourse of motherhood. Six of these mothers indicated that they practiced a parenting style that is child focused and/or that involves some aspects of attachment parenting. Lisa, for example, explained that she believed that mothers and fathers should focus their attention on the children for the first five years of life. Astrid wanted to be around her children a significant amount of time because this was important for their development and because she wanted to be there "to see them grow." Madelaine and Astrid mentioned Dr. Sears' *Attachment Parenting* (Sears and Sears,

2001) as the model for raising their children. All six women chose to have their children sleep with them for the first few years of their lives. Nancy explained that she needed them to be in her bed because she found this to be less disruptive to her sleep when the children needed to breastfeed or when they needed support with bad dreams or illness.

Resistance that Involves the Role of Mother

Not being responsible for all of my children's behaviours or how they turn out. All the women in the study stated that they did not feel responsible for how their children turned out. They acknowledged that they are one of many factors that influence their children's development. Lilith, for example, said: "And, 'cause, like, some studies are saying, the parents are actually, like, 13 percent of control over the future of the kids. I mean, that was the lowest number I saw, but that was the one I liked the best (laughs). I only have 13 percent of control." She explained that although she believed that there are other influences that impact children's development, she nevertheless made efforts to teach her daughters to act with respect and to be well behaved.

The other mothers shared similar stories, and believed that biology is a strong influence. For instance, Aibrean stated that her son had been diagnosed with Attention Deficit Hyperactive Disorder (ADHD) and that she did not feel responsible for his condition. Jane said, "Nature is so much ingrained, they will develop the way they are going to develop." Carla stated that, "Genetics are the canvas. The canvas can't be changed," but that, "how you are made to feel about yourself when you're a baby and a toddler by adults around you" is also an influence. Catherine said "genetics, nurture, love, environment" are all influences on who children are and who they become. Alexandra said, "It's a soup of factors." Kate said she did not take all the blame, but at the same time, she could not take the credit either: "I feel like I can't take the credit for how they turn out." Finally, Theo and Lisa stated that although they were not the only influences on their children, they saw themselves as very influential. Theo said, "the mother is a huge factor" in a child's life. Lisa said, "I take credit." These two women appeared to view themselves as more influential than the rest.

Not feeling loving toward my children all the time. A few of the mothers expressed that they did not feel loving towards their children all the time. Aibrean explained that when her first son was small she shared her frustrations with other mothers at a parent/baby group:

> *It's kind of a playgroup but much more organized. And ...*
> *I looked at the parents, and instructors, and I said, "You*
> *know, I don't like to be a mom all the time."...The idea*
> *that mothers are all wonderful and all loving is a myth. I*
> *mean, I think it is possible to love your child completely.*
> *It's completely possible to love your child unconditionally*
> *and to be loving, and not necessarily act in a loving way*
> *all the time. You know what I mean?*

Anna, Nancy, Astrid, and Theo found that children can be very difficult to care for at times and they acknowledged that they do not always feel loving towards their children. Theo chose to speak up about the difficulties and pain of taking care of an infant: "I'm pretty forthright that there was a lot of times when I didn't really like her."

Not cooking or cleaning as my main role. Several of the women explained that they did not view their role as that of a cook and/or cleaning person. Aibrean and Alice described how their mothers had focused too much of their energies on having perfectly clean homes and cooking fancy meals. They did not want to spend their time focused on these endeavours. Alice explained that she made sure that she had food that her children could prepare on their own or made nutritious meals such as sandwiches and raw vegetables: "So a lot of times, we'll have, you know, raw cut up vegetables, and toast and maybe some tofu, for supper.... Because I'm sorry, he's here all day, he eats eight times a day. I can't make eight meals a day. So I see my job as making sure that there are snacks that he can help himself to." Lilith and Lisa were not interested in cleaning and cooking; they did not see that as their contribution. Although Lisa explained that her parents were gourmet cooks and she wished she could cook that way for her daughter, however, she did not like nor was interested in it.

Not taking credit or blame. Kate's story yielded some instances of resistance that were unique to her. This may not mean that she was the only one resisting in this way, but rather that these facets were central to her story of resistance but not to the others'. Kate stated that she does not believe in sheltering her children from the outside world; she hoped that children could play outside without needing adult supervision. She did not believe in catering to her kids, who participated in the running of the home as equal participants and not just as helpers. She explained that, in this way, her children's Montessori school influenced her because there also they taught the children to be full participants rather than simply helpers. Finally, Kate's style of mothering was "to go with the flow"; she considered herself a "slack parent": "I'm very relaxed about lot of things that other parents ... get very stressed about...I'm a very slack parent."

Concluding Thoughts

The previous discussion illustrates that the women resisted several aspects of the dominant discourse of motherhood; they each resisted differently and to differing degrees. This suggests that resistance has many different faces, and that we cannot formulate one right way to resist. Rather, each mother will resist what makes sense to her. Something worth noting is that how the women resisted was unique to each of them. They all saw themselves as conscious about the social expectations on them, on how many of these expectations were oppressive to them, but also how many were not aligned with their own values. Furthermore, in aligning some of their resistance and maternal practices with their values, some of them appeared to be practicing intensive mothering. Those who chose to practice Attachment Parenting felt that they had little support to be able to care for their needs. They argued, however, that the problem was not being closely attached to their children, but that there weren't other relatives or invested adults sharing with them in the care of their children. What this highlights is that resistance has many faces and may not appear to the outside observer as resistance at all. We can then say that resistance may be in the eye of the beholder. Furthermore, resistance in every case led to a sense of empowerment, regardless of what or how they resisted. So, resistance regardless of its form was, in the case of all these women, experienced in a positive manner. Further analysis revealed what their experience of resistance was like. The following chapter presents the many facets of their experience.

Chapter 4

Resistance and Empowerment

You gain strength, experience, and confidence by every experience where you really stop to look fear in the face. You must do the thing you cannot do.
—Eleanor Roosevelt

RESISTANCE AGAINST ANY DOMINANT DISCOURSE will often mean facing disapproval. In other words, because society likes its members to conform to established norms and expectations, it will oppose those who step outside of what is expected. The findings of the study on resistant mothers revealed that the experience of resistance was very complex. Resisting was found to be an experience that was both rewarding and taxing for most of the mothers who participated in the study. All the women I interviewed encountered societal opposition to some of their mothering practices.

At the same time that they encountered this opposition, they found that being resistant translated into feelings of empowerment and more mastery over their lives. Thus, resistance to the dominant discourse of motherhood resulted in a sense of empowerment even when this was met with opposition from others in society.

Some researchers have indicated that resistance is important and that many mothers do try to find ways to cope with the pressures placed on them by society. For example, Natasha Mauthner (1999), who examined mothers' experiences of post-partum depression, suggested that agency and resistance are positive possibilities for mothers. She explained that mothers are not passive victims of social ideologies. She found that the women in her study were actively struggling with themselves, and the people and the social world around them. This struggle of resistance was more successful for those mothers whose expectations of themselves as mothers were not unrealistic and who were able to let go of some societal standards.

For example, some women resisted by modifying their picture of the good mother into a more realistic one that did not lead to heightened internal conflict. Mauthner's discussion suggested that mothers might resist by modifying their views of the good mother. This point has important implications because it suggests one possible way in which mothers may resist: by changing their the definitions of their roles as mothers.

The experience of resistance and mothering for the women I interviewed was laden with joys, sorrows, frustrations, satisfactions, integrity and confusion. Their stories begin to paint a picture of what it is like to resist and about the process of resistance, which is not a simple undertaking. Rather, it is complex and has many faces. Their attempts to integrate various discourses with their personal experiences appeared to be at the core of this complexity. Their stories suggest that mothers who resist have experiences that are often liberating and positive but sometimes can be conflictual and difficult.

In the study, I explored the following two questions: (a) what is the meaning and experience of mothering for women who are actively resisting the Western dominant discourse of motherhood? and, (b) how are these personal meanings and experiences grounded in these women's personal contexts as well as in dominant and alternative discourses and personal practices? The analysis was carried out in two parts. In answering the first research question, I identified the following themes illustrating these mothers' experiences of mothering. These themes include: (a) resisting is rewarding and liberating; (b) resisting entails juggling and balancing; (c) resisting entails ideological work, reframing, and reconciling; and (d) resisting involves some difficulties. Let's now turn our attention to how these women *experienced* the act of resistance to the dominant discourse of motherhood.

Experience of Mothering as Empowering, Rewarding, and Liberating

Empowering, rewarding, and liberating

All of the mothers I interviewed found that resisting against some of the societal expectations on them was rewarding and liberating. Resisting resulted in a sense of pride and conviction, in an experience of added freedom, in feelings of *empowerment* and integrity, in seeing their children doing well, and in feeling little or no guilt. Overall, these women felt good about the way they had chosen to mother. They felt convinced that the choices they made were the best for them and their children. In other words, they believed that the way they mothered benefited them, not only their children. These were the benefits of opposing the pressures that society placed on them to be perfect mothers. Anna said,

> I think there's the belief that there is one right way to be a parent.... But I think it's wrong, I think those expectations cause people anxiety and grief about their parenting. And they wouldn't have it if it wasn't for these standard norms everybody is trying or they are supposed to be meeting.

Conviction and pride

By questioning and making decisions on how to mother, these women experienced a sense of conviction and pride about their views and their choices around mothering. Mothering in their unique ways led them to feel empowered with a strong sense of integrity. This sentiment is captured well in the words of Lilith:

> I don't have the guilty mamma feeling, you know, I live by my convictions and I don't allow myself to fall into doing whatever everybody else says. And I don't guilt myself for the fact that I've gone out this weekend. I don't guilt myself for the fact that I did a homework assignment when I should have been playing with my kids. I do think that I am going to raise two of the coolest people, and that shows that I'm doing it right. I live by my convictions, and I am very proud of myself for that.

Conviction and commitment to their choices was central to their process of resistance. For these mothers, being convinced of their views and choices added to a sense of integrity in staying true to themselves. This conviction provided them with a foundation to continue to follow through with their choices even when they encountered challenges. Being convinced that what they chose was right for them led to feelings of pride for many of them. Anna's story invites reflection on this theme. At the time of the study, Anna had a twelve-year-old girl and a ten-year-old boy. She began her life as a mother with an infant who cried constantly, so that for Anna, mothering was not a positive experience initially. Anna explained that her first exposure to motherhood led her to continue to pursue her interests and her work because it was through these pursuits that she felt competent. Anna resisted by not being the only person to take care of her children, as she felt convinced about leaving them in the care of others. Anna did not feel indispensable; she rather believed in involving others in helping her children. Having others be involved freed her to pursue her career and her interests. Anna stated that mothering in a way that worked for her and not buying into social expectations "has been empowering." Anna did not believe that she had to follow all the social expectations on her as a mother. She tried to find a balance between what worked for her and for her children. She felt empowered because she made sure that she took care of her needs and herself as well as her children's in order to be what she considered a good mother. She said,

> *I have always thought it was the right thing to do. That my needs and my career and my happiness, if I was going to be a good mother, I have to fulfill that side of me ... and it's enabled me, I think, to have a higher quality of life than I would have had, because I am an individual too.*

Anna's experience is an illustration of the experience of many of the women. These women felt good about themselves as mothers. They expressed that mothering the way they had chosen to mother meant that they stayed true to themselves and to who they are. They felt grounded and in charge of their own path.

Being convinced about their choices helped these women remain committed to their mothering practices. For example, resistance comes with some challenges because women who rebel have to face criticism from others. This is never easy and it takes conviction to stay true to one's decisions and views. One of my convictions as a mother was to allow my girls to express their feelings and to create space for dialogue between us. This meant that their expressiveness often appeared too pushy or persistent or even rude. I heard from people in my family that I was doing it wrong and that my girls were overly attached to me. To this day I don't know if my view and my practices around this issue were right (who can?), but I stuck with what I believed was right because of my conviction. I wanted my daughters to have a voice and to feel like their thoughts and feelings were important. My 26-year-old often tells me that none of her friends are as open with their parents as she is with me. I feel blessed to be able to be a resource for her and her sister because it allowed me to be informed and involved in their lives during their youth. It does take conviction to do what one believes in in the face of societal opposition.

Some of the women I interviewed found that meeting their needs and mothering from a place of conviction enabled them to have a higher quality of life. Anna explained that mothering from conviction allowed her to feel better about her life and her mothering. Louise also explained that she was satisfied with leaving her children with friends or family while she traveled to competitions—as this was her passion—because she believed that others have "great wisdom" to offer her children. Louise explained that she felt "pretty good" about the way she had chosen to mother and she made choices that worked for her and her kids. When I asked why it is important for her to mother the way she did, she answered: "Well, I guess it is true to me. I don't know how to do it any other way. It has come from my essence. I've got my guiding light for me." In addition, Louise described how she does not allow the views and judgments of others to impact her experience. She explained that when she has experienced pressures from others she uses humor to handle it and does not let it bother her: "I don't judge myself by their points of view." In sum, the women I interviewed were convinced about many of the choices they had made. Although they still worried about their children, they realized that they could not possibly be perfect and they also had needs that were important. Knowing that they were making choices that made sense to them and being convinced about their beliefs led to feelings of pride and contentment for most of them.

Liberating

Furthermore, being convinced that they were not to blame for how their children turn out was experienced as liberating by these women. All the mothers felt that there are many other factors that impact children. This did not mean they were complacent about their children, but rather that they did not assume the burden of societal blame. By not taking on the full responsibility for all of their children's behaviours, personality, psychological problems, choices, and so on, these women felt freed from societal reproach. The idea that mothers can prevent all mishaps creates a huge burden and places mothers in a state of constant anxiety and self-doubt. These women were not invested in these myths and accepted that their children were going to be exposed to other influences regardless of their efforts. This, in turn, allowed them to continue to do the best mothering job they could within their own contexts without aspiring to be "perfect" mothers.

Self-esteem

Questioning the dominant discourse of motherhood and making their own choices enhanced these women's self-esteem. They stated that making alternative choices made them happy and that they felt good about themselves as mothers. They expressed that mothering their way meant that they stayed true to themselves and doing so was empowering. Anna's words exemplify how many of the women did not feel like they had to follow the social expectations on them as mothers. She explained that she felt empowered by her choices: "I had to take care of myself here...To me, it has been empowering." She explained that making the choice to pursue her work outside of the home and her interests were key in her having a good quality of life:

And it's enabled me, I think, to have a higher quality of life than I would have had ... because you only live one life and I have to ... be happy in that life. I have to mother the way I mother to be happy. And as I do that I am always balancing my happiness with theirs. In that way I have been able to continue what made me happy because in my view, it wasn't affecting them. As long as it wasn't adversely affecting them, it felt okay to do what I had to do.

My way is good for me and my children

All these mothers expressed feeling confident that the way they had chosen to mother was beneficial to their children. Catherine is a case in point. Catherine was 33 at the time of the interview. She had one daughter aged seven. She had been married to her partner, Jonathan, for twelve years. She worked for a financial company in a "male dominated" industry. They decided that Jonathan would stay home with their daughter while Catherine pursued her career. Jonathan runs his business from home. The following can summarize Catherine's views:

> *I love my daughter very much, but in order to be a good mother, I need to take care of myself and my career, I need to nurture my relationship, and I need to be a co-parent rather than her primary caregiver. It is only in balancing these aspects of my life that I can feel whole and fulfilled. This way of mothering works for me and my family.*

She explained that making the choices she had made was rewarding when she observed her daughter was "doing so well." Catherine was pleased about how her daughter was "turning out." She believed that "relinquishing" primary care to her partner was the right choice for her daughter. When I asked her, what she found rewarding about the way she had chosen to mother, she confidently replied,

> *Seeing her. (laughs) I think that's the big thing, just knowing that it didn't have to be me. Just relinquishing the primary care giving role, and I do believe that it was a better choice,*

it was a better choice. Yeah, she's thriving in every facet of her life. She loves school, she loves piano, she loves baseball, swimming. Like, she loves life. She's got aspirations. I mean she's seven and she's ... reading about many subjects. She wants to be a marine biologist. She has huge aspirations. So I, I think, we've accomplished that.

She believed that relinquishing primary care to her partner was beneficial not only to her career and her interests but to her daughter. Other women had similar experiences. Louise, for example, explained that she felt happy to see that her daughters were independent, team players. By modeling independence and expecting them to be part of the family team, she felt she had encouraged them to be strong, independent children. Their being independent, in turn, also allowed her to continue to pursue her interests: "It is not only independence in yourself, but is being able to contribute so that you are not a drag, you are never a drag on people."

In addition, many of the women felt that one of the rewards of mothering the way they had chosen to mother was the positive influence they were having on their children. In relation to this experience, Nancy said:

I guess I know ultimately that my children are going to be competent adults, competent employees, competent relationship partners by their experience of my husband's and my relationship with each other, and our relationship with them, as individuals and as parents. So I guess in general, what I find rewarding, is knowing that overall, they're getting a pretty damn good education in that area.

Aibrean—who identified herself as someone who questions what society has expected of her—emphasized that an important aspect of what is rewarding for her is that her son tends to ask questions rather than take what he's told as the only possible answer:

Andy says why a lot. When he does look at a situation, he has his own thoughts. Aside from what society has thrown down his throat, I would like to think that I am the one

*who has influenced him to do things like that. That's ex-
tremely rewarding.*

Lilith stated that the way she has chosen to mother is intended
to be a positive influence on her daughters:

*I figure that if it is right for me and my kids, it's good 'cause
I know I am doing a good job. The proof is in the pudding:
when you look at my kids you know I am doing a good
job. And that's the thing, I am doing a good job.*

For Jane, making sure that her children are exposed to her husband, other family members and to her, means that they will be
stronger, more flexible people:

*I guess I'm hoping that it will impact them by making them
stronger, I suppose, so that they have more experience with
different care givers, whatever that means, with different
people that love them. That they will be sort of more flexible because they've had different adult styles. But, you
know, they still will have had the structures set by myself
in conjunction with my husband and stuff.*

These women resisted because it was beneficial to them and their
own well-being. However, they did not resist without considering
the well-being of their children. The women in this study viewed
their children as resilient and independent thinkers. They certainly
felt that mothering entailed juggling between what they wanted
and needed and what their children needed.

Resistance allows me more freedom
These women also felt that mothering by resisting some of the
social expectations on them was liberating because it allowed
them to have more freedom. Taking care of their needs, eliciting
the support of others, or relinquishing some of their responsibilities to their partners was "like having the best of both worlds."
For example, Carla explained that parenting this way was easier
because she was able to do things she likes. She did not mind that

she was not her daughter's "main person." She explained, "It doesn't bother me when people think that...she's very comfortable with me too. I mean we are very close." For Carla, co-parenting and having her partner as the main caregiver is "easier than any other possible way because I get the best of both worlds, I get to be a cross between a mother and a father."

What this meant was that many of these women did not view themselves as indispensable caregivers in their children's lives, they did not believe that it had to be the mother who solely cares for all the needs of children. A good example is Lilith's story. She was a single mom of two toddlers. She was 23 years old and a student at a local college. Two years prior to our interview, she only had a 10th grade education. She was committed to her children and to herself equally. By the time I met with her, she was on her way to completing a university degree. In order to do this, she placed her kids in full-time daycare. She expressed that she loved her daughters but as a person she needed other things in her life outside of mothering such as school, fun, or activism. She explained that staying at home would "drive me crazy" and she did not find it stimulating enough. By involving others, doing activities she enjoyed, and taking time for herself, she felt a certain level of freedom and she knew that she was doing what was right for both herself and her daughters. She enthusiastically said,

> I do go on dates, I'm a single parent! But I'm also 23, I'm a 23 year-old! So I mean, I go out on weekends at least one night a week, generally both. And I mean I go out and I have fun ... and I go to the bar and dance, and I mean, people just see that as being selfish.... I get my kids in the morning and I feel refreshed, I feel rejuvenated. Like I've gotten to be 23, now I can be a mommy, you know. And I mean, I don't see it as, I see it as me taking care of myself, because when you take care of yourself, you are better able to take care of other people.

It is important to note that for those women who were willing to give up the main caregiver role and who experienced this freedom, relinquishing this role was conditional to the alternative caregiver being someone who was emotionally invested in their child. All of the women who have partners or husbands who took on the main caregiving role, except for Alexandra, did not agree with taking their children to daycare. This is significant because having partners who are involved allows them to pursue their interests or work without having to resort to leaving their children at daycare. In other words, they preferred to have one parent or someone who is a close, loving adult be with their children.

Relief and integrity

These women did not give credence to the idea that mothers must pretend that the experience of being a mother is always good. They recognized that mothering has its dark side and many chose not to be silent about it. They found that by voicing the negative aspects of motherhood to others they felt relief and a sense of integrity. About half the mothers found relief in voicing to others that they did not like motherhood all the time or that they did not like their children all the time. Nancy's story is a useful illustration of how some mothers found it helpful to voice to others that they dislike their children at times. Nancy was 46 at the time of the interview and she had three children aged 16, 12, and eight. She described that when she was pregnant with her first child, she met three pregnant social workers with whom she became close. She explained that she felt fortunate to have contact with those women:

> *Because any of the times that I felt that what I wanted to do was to kill my child, just murder her, she was crying or whatever, I would pick up the phone and call one of these three women and say, "I want to throw this kid out the window (I lived in a fifth floor of a building) and jump out myself!" And they would scream back on the phone: "Not you, first me, then you could do it!" And so I was very lucky that I had this kind of outlet for the expression of that kind of rage.... I was able to do it because I knew these were other people who were coming from similar backgrounds, professional backgrounds. They would understand that if I was saying that, there*

was no need to pick up the phone and call the ministry, so it was safe to do, and it was also the way to express it and then know that there was somebody else to hear it, and then I could go on and deal with whatever had to be dealt with.

Gradually, Nancy said she learned that it was "okay" to have some negative feelings towards her children,

Now, I remember initially feeling really guilty, that here is my little infant kid, screaming and crying, needing me. I just want to … and I feel really intense rage, I want to sleep, I need to sleep, I don't want to give you the breast, I don't want to give you anything. Just shut the fuck up and let me sleep! And what I noticed around me, with the exception of those women who were my friends, is that to make any acknowledgment of any negative feeling was not acceptable. Ah, and I knew, that if I kept that stuff in me, that wouldn't be right.

Nancy explained that she acknowledges that sometimes she could do better or different but that she did not feel guilty anymore, so she learned to take action and to question what she can do better next time. Nancy stressed the importance of speaking about the negative aspects of being a mother and raising children. She explained that when she first became a mother she noticed that to acknowledge any negative feeling regarding her children or her experience of mothering was not acceptable. But she also recognized that she had to be who she was and speak up. She also said that when you become a mother nobody tells you that it feels like a "vacuum cleaner on your breast, the kid does something where it is going to hurt, or that you won't want to do it at times or that you are exhausted at times." For Nancy it was very important to speak up about those aspects of her experience because it allowed her to share with others and know that she was not "nuts or bad." Nancy emphasized that being able to speak about her difficulties helped her to go on and not bottle it up inside. This was a very important value for Nancy. She was not willing to silence her feelings and views even when she encountered others who were judgmental toward her or uncomfortable with her words: "well, giving voice, not just when people agreed, but also, you know, not censoring, knowing that there was people for whom this was a discomfort."

Other women in the study shared very similar stories. They all experienced anger at their infants or toddlers from time to time and were vocal about it with others. Some of them encountered support while others encountered negative reactions from others. When Aibrean expressed her feelings about not liking to be a mom all the time in her mother/play group, she found that some mothers reacted negatively and left the room angry and disapprovingly. But others were supportive of her feelings; they agreed that being a mom sometimes is very difficult. Aibrean felt validated when the group leader normalized the experience for her: "Yeah, parenting isn't exactly always fun." She felt that this experience freed her to be able to acknowledge that she doesn't always like being a mom: "Okay, I don't have to love this all the time." All these women found it helpful to speak to others about the negative aspects of being a mother. They reached out to friends who understood them, which allowed them to vent their frustrations, rage, and anger, and in turn helped them feel they had the integrity to not continue to sell to other mothers the idea that mothering is always wonderful.

Speaking out did have a downside, which is to be expected in a society that highly discourages alternative mothers' voices. Many of these women explained that they often felt judged and this made it difficult to be transparent with some people. This speaks to the challenges that uncovering "the mask" (Maushart, 2000) may have for mothers. It is not our children's fault, or our fault that there are aspects of this job that are unpleasant. There are children who sleep poorly, are argumentative, sensitive or highly emotional, or who have disabilities, are overly hyper, restless, uncooperative, and so on. It is impossible to love everything about our children or about the job of being a mother. The dominant discourse of motherhood tells mothers to negate their feelings and sacrifice for the children and yet mothers should have a right to honour and acknowledge their feelings and their negative experiences. Susan

Maushart's book, *The Mask of Motherhood*, emphasizes this point; mothering is not all fun and games, but society expects mothers to keep that information secret and only show joy and happiness to the world (2000). The mothers in the study found that speaking up was beneficial to them and in some cases they felt strongly that mothers should speak up because this would be supportive of other mothers.

Less or no guilt

Most of the women in the study either did not mention guilt as part of their experience, or explicitly voiced that maternal guilt is not significant for them. For example, as I mentioned earlier, Lilith explained that she does not have the "guilty mamma" feeling; she goes out on weekends, pursues an education, and does not clean incessantly. For the most part, she emphasized that she does *not* feel guilty and that she is proud of her choices because she is guided by her convictions. She said, "It is very easy to guilt a mom, you know, it's very easy to do that ... I don't have as many of those days now that I get rid of my kids and do things on a regular basis." Lilith's words speak to the possibility that mothers can escape feeling guilty. She did say that society places a guilt trap on mothers and she sometimes fell into that trap but always caught herself and got herself out of it. Lilith was convinced that she had the *right* to have fun and to be an individual so that when she engaged in meeting her needs, she did not feel guilty because she had claimed it as her right.

Jane also resisted by not believing that she has to be present all the time. She feels free to be away and she does not feel guilty about this. She explained,

> But I don't feel like I have to be there all the time micro-managing or doing everything. I feel like I'm ridding myself from a lot of that guilt that ... whereas I know other mothers feel they have to be there all the time.

Jane resolved the experience of guilt by including her partner as a co-parent. In the case of other women, the actual experience of mothering helped them to rid themselves of maternal guilt. Nancy, for example, described how the journey through motherhood taught her that she does not have to feel guilty. She explained that initially, she felt guilty when she was angry with her baby because she would cry non-stop:

> *Do I think at times that I can do better or differently? Yeah, but I use the opportunities to think about what that looks like. What I can learn from this, and not. I don't sit down with, 'I feel so guilty, or I'm so bad!' Rather, okay, I was a bitch mother from hell this morning, how can I do better next time?*

Many of the women I interviewed had experienced guilt early on. The findings of the study illustrate some of the struggles that mothers experience in endeavouring to make sense of the contradictions between their experiences and the social expectations on how mothers should act and feel. Many of these mothers, who mentioned experiencing guilt, only experienced it early in their lives as mothers. Making alternative choices was a struggle because they faced opposition around them. Catherine, who chose to relinquish the main caregiving role to her partner, observed,

> *I think there is an element in society that if you are not present ... that there's an element of guilt surrounding that as well. And I think a lot of people impose that on mothers as, well, huge guilt.... I initially felt guilty leaving her with someone else. So we came to an agreement that we did not want someone else to raise her... I felt terribly guilty initially [leaving her with her dad], and people were telling me that it was wrong. That how could you leave her, including our family—his parents, my father—what are you doing? He's not capable of raising a child. You know blah, blah, blah. And you know, I said, I just don't accept that. I don't believe that's true. I've seen him in action and he's calm and he's patient.*

Catherine dealt with her initial guilt by not accepting the judgment of others and observing her husband's qualities as a parent.

To expand on this last point, it is worth stating that two of the mothers were exceptions in that they did experience guilt. Alexandra explained that she felt guilty not only in relation to her mothering but also around her professional work because she felt she never did enough for her daughter. She said, "I feel guilty much of the time because my work has taken up a lot of my energy in the last eight years...the fact that I don't love my work...somehow makes it worse that I have expended so much energy on it rather than on my daughter." Lisa said, "I have a lot of guilt." She explained that she is aware that "that's stupid" but that she still feels very guilty mainly because she recently separated and is depriving her daughter from the opportunity to live in an intact family. It appears that in both of these cases, although Lisa and Alexandra resisted by questioning many aspects of the discourse, they complied with other aspects. For example, they believed that mothers should not use up all their energy at work and that they should preserve the family unit.

Nevertheless, the fact that only two of the mothers expressed feeling maternal guilt suggests that resistance can be a protective factor against guilt. Guilt arises when we feel we are doing something wrong, and every mother makes mistakes. What helped many of the women I interviewed was that they believed that it is impossible to be perfect; they believed that children develop because of a variety of factors beyond the way they are mothered and are inherently resilient. Some of the factors they identified as influencing children are biological/innate characteristics, peers, media, teachers, personal struggles and problems, and the presence of extended family.

In sum, these women found that resisting the dominant discourse was rewarding in many ways, and particularly in a lessened experience of maternal guilt due to a feeling of conviction in the choices they made. However, as was apparent in some of their comments, this process although rewarding, also entailed juggling and balancing. The following section illustrates how this juggling was partly due to the women's belief that only someone invested in their child should take over a caregiving role and to weighing the harm or benefit associated with any given choice they made. In other words, freedom was contingent upon knowing that their children were loved, safe, cared for, and turning out well.

Juggling and Balancing

Achieving balance is a struggle

All the women in the study believed, to different degrees, that meeting their needs was important. This often meant that they had to struggle to balance meeting their needs and the needs of their children. They juggled a variety of tasks in an effort to meet both their own needs and those of their children. It was important to them to maintain the balance. These women indicated that, by meeting their own needs, they could find contentment. They believed that if they were happy or content, their children would have a greater chance of happiness as well. Jane felt she had to be good to herself. If she meet her needs and was strong and well, she could be a better mother. She said that by doing what she wants to do, she was a better mother:

> *Yeah, I find that when I am all in one or all in the other [side of the balance], I am just not happy. It drives me totally mad, actually...If I can't be good to myself, it just kind of ... all the walls come tumbling down.... So for me it's imperative, to be the kind of mother that I want to be, to not be a mother all the time. I guess that sums up a lot of my beliefs about mothering.*

Although they made sure that they attended to their needs, these moms expressed that it was important for them not to hurt their children in the process. They made efforts to take the well-being of their children into account when making decisions. This led to the struggle of balancing between their needs and their children's. For example, Louise found that following through with making choices that worked for her meant constant juggling because her partner traveled all the time. The juggling involved an exploration of the choices available to her, and of being attentive to not only her needs but her children's and her partner's needs too. She explained:

> *So you know it's a constant shuffling. Then, when I finish school, will I be able to turn it into something that is, you know, contributing to our family, and if I do that, am I*

going to take away from my kids? You know because, our rhythms, are only by the school year, they are not by my mate's job. I mean, he doesn't work a nine to five job, he's either gone or he's here. Will I be able to remember my scenario? So you know it's a constant shuffling.

Resistance entailed some turmoil

Several of the women in the study experienced turmoil and felt they were constantly facing contradictions. Although they experienced these struggles they did not experience them to the same degree. Astrid was 30 years-old at the time of the interview. She was an artist and a stay-at-home mom of two children, a boy who was three-and-a-half years old and a girl who was eight months old. She was very involved as a La Leche League leader, she led parenting study groups, and she was an activist. Astrid emphasized that she was not willing to compromise her beliefs or her integrity and that she was determined to take actions that "compromise" oppressive conditions. She said, "I challenge expectations about mothers by refusing to be pitted against my children and refusing to settle for the world as it is." She did not buy into what she called the "cult of materialism" or the ideologies inherent in striving for material success and career. She, therefore, had chosen not to work for money; she believed that mothers should raise their children in a community—which she lacked—and she did not believe that a mother should have to do it all. At the same time, she was unable to have a positive experience because she saw society as oppressive and not providing mothers with opportunities for community and support. The gist of her experience can be summarized as follows:

I have encountered many contradictions, limitations (isolation, lack of support and community, judgment), and pressures as a parent. This has created turmoil in me. I have decided that what is most liberating to me is to jump into those areas that are supposed to be most oppressive to me and stick to my beliefs. The way I mother works for us even though I have to make some compromises because the social supports are not there.

This statement illustrates what many mothers may experience in society. Astrid's words represent the experience of mothers who realize that the problems they face are not their fault but related to a society that does not support mothers or children. She felt that society views mothers who stay home with their children in contradictory ways and this caused her turmoil. She explained that staying home with her children puts her in:

...a dichotomous position ... because I am staying home to take care of my children, and so even though I'm aware of some of these myths, I'm very conscious of the fact that people [judge me] according to those things. For the most part I will be viewed as somebody who has fallen for the myth of the perfect mother, so to speak. "Oh, yeah, she's at home with the kids, she's really just a doormat, she has sacrificed so much for the kids." So, I guess, it's difficult for me to find venues, or the opportunity to actually position myself and say, "You know, I'm staying at home with my kids. And I'm doing that because I believe in it, and it works for us." But on the other hand, I am not a doormat, and I'm not doing it because I have lots of money or something. What I have found is that staying at home has put me most often feeling resentful, because I am doing it, on my own! Ah ... I guess I take that responsibility, because I have chosen to stay home. But on the other hand it really rips me off during the day when I just think, god, does it have to be this hard for me to find another woman for me to just go over and, you know, "take my kids for three hours, I've got to do something," and that kind of thing.

This quote communicates how Astrid experienced turmoil and how she was impacted by the lack of social supports and community. Her experience illustrates how the dominant discourse of motherhood limits how many mothers experience judgment. In Astrid's case, staying home but in isolation from other mothers and the larger community was problematic for her: she wanted to be around her kids and enjoy them but the lack of support created a situation where she didn't have time independent from her children. Her struggle to come to terms with the burdens that the dominant discourse of motherhood placed on her was aggravated by the realization that her work as a mother was not considered work. She expressed this to me with such conviction and power that I would like to honour her words by including them here:

> As a stay-at-home mom, many people believe that I do not work. Not only is caregiving for one's own children not recognized as work, but the related activities and interests that I pursue tend to be volunteered and, therefore, they are not seen as work. Unless one makes money, it is generally understood that one is engaged in some kind of leisure activity ... I see this as one of the most debilitating and demeaning myths of our culture. There is also the perception that I am not a strong woman because I stay home with my kids, i.e., I am a doormat who sacrifices herself for the well-being of her kids. On the contrary, I am a fiercely strong woman. I do not sacrifice myself in any way. I make many compromises because that is absolutely required in taking care of children....
>
> The bottom line is this: whether a woman works at home taking care of her kids or works outside of the home away from her kids, she is heavily oppressed by patriarchy. The only conclusion that I can come to then is to overturn patriarchy. No small feat indeed, but I continue to believe in my ability to make small but significant contributions. My resistance is refusing to sacrifice my child's interests because the world tells me I must do so if I am to be liberated. It is the engine of patriarchy that must be sacrificed. I create a world for myself and my kids that does not heed to patriarchy. I insist upon it ... the problem is not being with your children; it is being with your children in isolation from others; it is being with our children all the time; it is having to choose between the two; it is not having a good enough child care alternative; it is not having a community of caregivers

who are emotionally vested in our children (rather than financially); it is living in a society that does not value or support mothers' mothering.

These are the things that must give away, not my interests, not my child's. So although I choose to stay home where I am indeed isolated and lonely, unsupported, bored, solely responsible and undervalued, I take responsibility for my choice to stay home and I do what I can do to change those things. I stay at home with the confidence that I have not accepted the unacceptable choice of honouring my kids' needs or honouring my own. I honour both.

Astrid's story illustrates that resistance is not related to being employed and pursuing a career. She resisted by not pursuing a career just to give her children more material goods at the expense of not spending time with them. She stated that mothers who stay at home become isolated and lonely because the social structure does not allow for community and support amongst parents. Astrid has experienced turmoil because her choice to honour her children and stay home with them meant that she has to do it all by herself, and she sometimes finds this boring and isolating. Astrid's willingness to voice her boredom is an aspect of her resistance. She does not blame the children; she blames social structures: while mothers are expected to be ever-present for their children, no one is available as respite, or support; the job becomes monotonous, boring, and isolating. What Astrid points out is that societal institutions and myths are responsible for many aspects of mothers' struggles. Astrid experienced frustration because she perceived that her isolation and loneliness were related to oppression. Astrid also resisted by being a social activist:

I am a social activist. In this I challenge the mainstream cult of individualism, the move toward conservatism, and the belief that economic well-being is a prerequisite to happiness. This area, social activism, is where I think I vent a lot of my frustration about being a mother in this society.... Directing my frustration out of the house and into the public realm seems to be a way of coping.

Madelaine's story also illustrates the challenges and turmoil that mothers face when trying to live by their own values. Madelaine was 36 at the time of the interviews. She had two boys, six and ten years old. She was a writer/editor who worked from home for a few years and just recently had returned to working at an office. She had been involved in a women's organization as a researcher and writer on the topic of mother's work as work. She chose to stay home with her children while continuing to write from home. For Madelaine, mothering was a balancing act between pursuing her writing career, taking care of her needs, meeting the needs of her kids who were very important to her, and attending to her relationship. She experienced conflict between her alternative views on women and mothering and the societal pressures placed on her to mother in mainstream ways. She found her experience as a mother difficult in a society that is judgmental and that expects her to forget herself in the name of caring for her children. Madelaine viewed societal forces as part of the problem for mothers:

> *Well, a lot of attitudinal change needs to take place. I think that our interpretations are very traditional even though we want to believe on some level that they are not. And then of course there's day care; day care is not very accessible. There's not enough day care and it's too expensive for many people, and there's the way the workplace is set up such that, you know, it's hard to get a good paying part-time job that will allow you to balance your life. You know, the expectations that you will be able to be there at nine or nine to five or whatever the hours of the job, that there will be no interruption after you get there. That's one thing that at least has gotten better for me, and that's not accessible for everybody. Students don't get maternity leave, so all those kinds of infrastructures.*

Madelaine's words indicate her view that part of her experience is affected by social structures and not by self-deficiency. Furthermore, Madelaine suggested that she felt torn between taking care of her needs—which she believes are important—and taking care of her children's needs. She went on to say, "But it's difficult you know, I want to be there when they are not in school, and yet I also want to do these things." For Madelaine, the lack of social supports and recognition that mothers' work is work, and her understanding of women's issues all interact to make her experience difficult:

So I struggle with the notion of, do I think of motherhood as being work in the sense that, work is work, or is it somehow separate from being a writer and being a researcher and all of that? And it's hard to integrate it. Even though I spent all those years researching and writing about it and talking about mothering as work. And for me, I have never been able to relate, I don't believe that. But I'm affected by the negative feedback I get about that. People don't understand that. They don't really like it. They still see mothering or parenting as something that is completely separate from what you do in the rest of the world. And at kind of another level, I don't agree with that, I think that it's not healthy. And it's led to the structures in society that we have that make it hard for parents to be the parents they want to be. And yet I can't stand up and ... you know ... I don't think it has to be the mother who is there all the time.

A lot of children would benefit by not being with their mother. You know, it's just a person who really cares about them, or a person or group of people should be there. But it's hard. I mean, again the notion that mothers should be the one, that mother care is the best care and yet mothers should be out working. And this conflicts with the idea that mothers should contribute financially to the family. So there is this tension in values that are common in the U.K., Canada, and the U.S. People believe both of those things equally, mothers should look after children and they should contribute financially. So it's hard to hold those two. You know, we all hope to one degree or another.

It's hard, it's hard when it pits women against each other. You know, the women who put their kids in day

*care because they really like their job or because they really
need the money or some combination of those two things
versus women who have decided to be home. They kind
of suddenly are on opposite sides of the fence. Regardless
of what they believe, one way or the other they kind of
get pushed around into one of those, defending their own
choices. It's hard because I don't want to be critical of
someone else's choice.*

Sound familiar? Societal pressures and ideologies are a huge part
of why mothers struggle so much. Mothers receive contradictory
messages that leave them struggling to figure out what the best
course of action is for them and feeling like they are failing in one
realm or another.

There were many other things that concerned the women I
interviewed. The educational system, the medical system, the
fact that society does not include children so that parents rarely
have the option to go to gatherings or events with their children.
What came out of my analysis is that these women did a lot of
thinking and had developed a keen eye for the factors that affected their lives as mothers. They were not necessarily focused
on what they lacked or on whether they were deficient in their
parenting, but rather on how societal factors such as the mothering ideology, lack of community, pressures to be perfect, and
contradictory messages they received affected their lives in often
negative ways.

Facing many questions

Although these women expressed conviction and commitment to
mothering their way, the process was not always simple. It called
for the resolution of many questions surrounding what was right
for themselves and their family. At times they felt torn and found
it challenging to balance both demands. In choosing to mother in
a way that worked for them, these women found that they had
to consider many factors. Their decisions were not automatic but
rather entailed thought and reflection. Trying to evaluate each situation and deciding how to meet both their own and their children's
needs was sometimes difficult.

A good example of this challenge is illustrated in Theo's story. Theo experienced turmoil because she was very interested in her field and completing her Ph.D. She explained that in her view she needed to be more than a mother, but that at that point in her daughter's life it was very stressful to pursue other needs. Theo said, "I feel damned if I do and damned if I don't." At the time of our interview, Theo was deciding whether to continue her Ph.D. or to quit. She felt torn between her familial obligations and her love for her work.

Being able to achieve this balance seemed to be related to the age of their child. Some explained that the younger the child, the more difficult it was to take care of their own needs, but that as children got older it became easier. Carla said, "I think it's challenging when you have a newborn or a small infant in front to get that time to take care of yourself." Many of these mothers explained that when their children were very young, they sometimes had to wait to address their needs because more immediate needs had to be met for the child such as feeding, diaper changing, or providing comfort. Others explained that they did not have a community to support them so that when their partners were away at work, they were unable to attend to their needs for space and time.

Balancing between selflessness and "selfishness"

For the women in this study, this process became one of balancing between being "selfish" and being "selfless" and was impacted by the presence of supports such as community support, partner collaboration, flexible employment, support from extended families, and access to information. Like Astrid noted, the problem may not be being home with children, it may be that mothers lack supports and community so that they can have more balance and freedom in their lives. Her feelings may be how many mothers feel. The women in the study who had husbands who were very involved, or family or friends who were supportive, were able to meet their needs more easily than those who did not. Furthermore, those women who were the most content and who experienced the least guilt were those who had been able to rely on the consistent collaboration from partners, family, and/or friends.

Catherine's story illustrates this point well. Catherine chose to pursue a career in a male dominated and demanding field while her husband stayed home with their daughter. She said, "It's pretty good, I feel like I've got the best of everything." Having supports made it easier for these women to practice self-care. When children are in infant or toddler stages they may need more attention than when they are in elementary or high school. But, as I reported earlier, some mothers have shared with me that they don't even have time to shower or tidy up their home or let alone do things for themselves because they spend every minute with their baby/ child. They wait for their husband to come home to relieve them of the children because the discourse tells them they need to be dedicated, present, and avoid hurting their children.

Even though these women hold a conviction that taking care of themselves by meeting their own needs is their right, they found it difficult to put this value into practice. This process was one of struggling to balance between taking care of their children and pursuing what was important to them. In order to make sense out of their experiences and to make sensible choices, these women engaged in a process of questioning, researching, and pondering various options and discourses.

Ideological Work, Reframing, and Reconciling

The experience of mothering for these women was strongly co-loured by a process of ideological work, reframing, and reconciling conflicting social ideologies and discourses with their present and past experience. I selected the term ideological work to illustrate the process of thinking and questioning that these women engaged in. I borrowed from the concept of ideological work used by Sharon Hays (1996) and Alison Sears (2001) in that it provides a way to conceptualize the thinking work that mothers engage in when try-ing to reconcile competing and contradicting social beliefs.

The women I interviewed expressed that their experience of mothering had often been contrary to what they were told it would be. This contradiction initially left them feeling incompetent or with self-doubt. For example, Anna explained that following social norms was impossible with her first child who was very demanding and cried constantly. She was unable to apply what she had read in parenting books, so she had to find ways to feel competent outside of motherhood. Anna described how her first exposure to motherhood compelled her to question if she could be a full-time mother. This questioning process led her to conclude that she needed to continue to pursue her interests and her work because it was through these pursuits that she felt competent. Anna decided to end her maternity leave much earlier than planned and returned to work. After pondering over what was best for her, she felt convinced that leaving her child in the care of others was what was best for her.

In a similar vein, Alice also expressed that being completely immersed in motherhood was not as fulfilling as she had expected it to be. After careful consideration, she had to start writing again and focus more on her own needs even if it meant not spending all of her time being a mother. She felt that if she did not change the way she was mothering she would become "clinically depressed." Alice explained:

> My feeling about [having to take care of my needs] is that it was do or die. Like I had to do that, or I was going to become clinically depressed. It was almost like [motherhood] was only the torso in my life. But I also have these important limbs that also need exercise. I felt like I was cutting them off, which was not helping my torso at all, you know what I mean? And so, I felt that I had to [go back to my writing].

Strategizing

For most of the mothers in this study, questioning and critiquing societal expectations also led to strategizing about what to say and to whom, and about who should take care of their children. Many of these mothers experienced anger at their infants or toddlers from time to time and questioned whether to express this to others. Many chose to be vocal about it to challenge the expectation that mothering is always a positive experience. Some of them encountered support whereas others encountered negative reactions from others.

On the other hand, some of the women strategized by choosing to silence their views and experiences around certain people to avoid judgment or criticism. For example, Alice did not appreciate others judging the way she had chosen to mother. She explained that most of these alternative choices were made after researching and considering various options:

> *I chose not to vaccinate. That was a major one, I was so surprised at the people that came at me for that: doctors, giving me lectures about "stewardship" as a parent, how they are not my children. You know, they are my, "I am the steward of these people, and I owe it to them to," so on and so forth.*

Alice explained that her own family had been a major source of criticism about her choices. She had found also that in order to avoid judgment, she had to strategize how she acted, which in turn led to what she called "strategic friendships." She said, "I'm not sort of sitting in my life, going, why do I feel so alone (in a quiet voice). I *know* why. Because these strategic friendships that I have, that I have to have, I have no patience for them." What Alice meant is that she could not be herself or fully open with her friends, she had to strategize as to what was safe to say and what wasn't; that is why she called them "strategic friendships." For Alice the fact that others have judged her in the past and may judge her in the future had led her to become silent and distant, and therefore, isolated.

The mothers in my study also strategized about who should take care of their children. Most resisted the discourse that suggests that it is the mother who should be present at all times. Many of them chose to share, to different degrees, their caregiving responsibilities. Carla, for example, believes that having other loving adults who are willing to help with the care of her daughter, is important. For those who knew that they did not want to be the main caregivers of their children, exploring the best alternative meant resisting the idea that the mother should be the primary caregiver but it also meant finding an "acceptable" substitute. Some women, in contrast, resisted the anti-daycare myth and felt that daycare providers can be great contributors to their children's lives.

To conclude, the women engaged in a process of questioning and reconciling contradictions that affected their experience. They challenged many of the tenets of the dominant discourse of motherhood and struggled to make meaning out of their beliefs and their experiences by questioning and pondering their own best course of mothering.

Resistance Involves Some Difficulties

The process of resistance had a dark side. Many of the women who spoke to me found that it created challenges with others that led them to feel isolated, judged, or silenced. In order to manage these difficulties, they strategized and engaged in further ideological work.

Isolation

Some of the women in the study also spoke of feeling isolated. Lisa, a 33-year-old gay, single mother of a four-year-old girl, found that the hardest thing for her was the isolation that she had to endure. She felt torn between the pressure to choose between pursuing what is important to her and being with her child and she therefore sought to combine the two. She described how she lost some friends after she had a child: "I lost friends who unfortunately seemed to pick sides, you know. So that was a very difficult time because all of a sudden I was very isolated!" She explained,

> *The isolation is the worst one. For me what is missing is resources, resources, resources! I think I'm fairly self-sufficient. What are you supposed to do, walk up to someone on the street, "Hi you look like a nice person, would you like to be my friend? Would you like to talk about politics and raise our kids together?" No you don't. So resources, resources, resources.*

Lisa found it difficult to find friends who wanted to discuss topics that did not relate to their mothering or their children. She missed talking to others about other challenging topics. Even though she did have some friends, Lisa explained that they either had children, which made it difficult to co-ordinate getting together without the children, or they did not have children and this meant that she did not have the choice to bring her daughter along. For Lisa, the lack of community was at the core of her struggle. Like Astrid, she did not believe that her choices were the problem, but rather the way society is structured and the lack of commitment it has toward children and mothers.

Judgment and Criticism

Other women who felt isolated explained that making alternative choices around their mothering placed them under the scrutiny of others. They explained that finding like-minded parents was a challenge. Some of the women in the study felt that this type of judgment pressured them into isolating themselves. I don't think that these experiences are unique to mothers who resist; all of us experience this lack of societal recognition and support. The fact that many women can identify with it is evidence that it is a systemic phenomenon.

All of the women I interviewed expressed that they had felt questioned or judged by others, at least partially because they mothered in ways that contradicted the dominant discourse of motherhood. Alice's story is a relevant example of this theme. Alice was a 31-year-old mother of two (three and seven year olds). She had been married for eight years. Alice chose to have home births, practice extended breastfeeding, home-school her children, and raise them with a vegetarian diet. She spoke to her children about most topics openly and taught them about important social issues regardless of their age. Alice had to stop sharing her views with others in order to avoid judgment and criticism from them. It was very important for her to maintain good relationships with other parents so that her children could continue to have playmates. But she did not like being judged for the way she had chosen to par-ent her children. She highlighted her own family as being a loud, critical voice: "I feel like my family is the embodiment of society and they are frowning on me." She also shared that she did not like being judged, "cause I don't want the judgment, and I don't want to get on the podium for them."

Other women shared similar stories. Lilith, for example, explained that she had experienced significant judgment because she is a single mother. She described how strangers had either criticized her or called the Ministry of Children and Families: "When I had my kids, they figured that I needed help, so they opened a file on me." She went on to say,

> *You know, and I never really agree with anybody, but I am being challenged kind of by everybody.... And that's the thing, people think that because I'm by myself, I can't do the job of two parents. And that's right, I can't do the job of two parents. But I can be the best one damn parent that anyone has ever seen!*

Lilith also indicated that she had been "getting flak" from people for taking her kids to a demonstration about government cuts. She believed that it was necessary to explain to them that certain social issues affect them. Lilith felt that she dealt with people's opinions and judgments on an ongoing basis so that she has had to reaffirm with herself that she was on the right mothering path: "And for me, I deal with a bunch of people saying, 'you're doing this right, you're doing this wrong, you're doing this right,' but I know in my heart I'm doing this right, and that's all that matters." Lilith had experienced frustration from having to deal with the opinions of others, "I would not necessarily call them sorrows as much as frustrations, 'cause I just find that people's view points are really frustrating: people's opinions and their ability to argue their opinions without any fact."

Others also felt questioned and frustrated with having to explain themselves. This became very tiring and annoying. They felt they always had to justify themselves, so in many cases dealing with this became difficult. For instance, Alice and Aibearn stated that they do not like having to educate other people and explain their choices. Aibearn said,

> *I do feel questioned, I do get questions. I feel questioned. I feel like I should explain myself. I put the pressure on myself. Like, I need to educate people as to why I'm making these choices so they don't think I'm a bad person, or I*

*need to educate people on why I make these choices so that
maybe I can help them. I don't want to educate everybody,
I'm too freaking lazy to educate everybody.*

Many others felt frustrated that society expected them to feel
and behave a certain way when their experience was completely
different. These women stated that having others pressure them
or criticize their choices has affected them. For instance, Theo had
chosen to surround herself with like-minded friends, while Alice
and Madelaine had chosen to avoid conversations related to their
choices. Catherine experienced self-doubt initially. However, as the
years passed, she saw herself and her daughter doing so well, that
she was very satisfied with her choices to relinquish the primary
parenting role to her partner.

Finally, there were some who stated that they had experienced
judgment and criticism but this type of experience was not significant for them. When one hears these stories, it is clear that mothers
endure a lot of judgment from the constant scrutiny from others.

Silencing

Different women dealt with judgment in different ways. There
were a few who ended up feeling they had no choice but to "go
underground" or become silenced. These women found that sharing their views with certain others meant encountering judgment,
conflict, or the loss of potential friendships. In order to avoid conflict
or judgment, they chose to become silent about their views with
certain people. For instance, Alice explained that she had found
that some disagreed with the fact that she did not vaccinate her
children or that she gave birth at home, and some even distanced
themselves or became judgmental:

*Yeah, and I'm really careful about it. I don't go out into
groups with other mothers and talk about my choices,
and birth, or vaccination, or diet, or anything like that ...
I generally don't talk to people about it because I don't
want the judgment and I don't want to get on the podium
for them.... And so it is a little bit isolating, making different decisions. 'Cause you have to hide a part of yourself,*

you know. And it's a little bit isolating to do something at home.... I can't tell people all the stuff I am telling you because it's, you know, inappropriate in normal conversation, and you know, it gets in the way of my kids.... And it's hard to pick and choose amongst my friends.

Alice chose to not share her views so that her children wouldn't lose their playmates. She found that by choosing to home-school her children, she had to make efforts to find playmates for them. The price she believed she had to pay was to silence herself in regards to her parenting views so as to avoid conflict or the loss of those friendships for her children. This resulted in Alice having few close friends and feeling isolated.

Madelaine also chose to be silent to avoid conflict but also to avoid sounding judgmental of other mothers:

Partly if you don't want to be criticized, you don't want to engage in a conflict situation with somebody.... Because everybody is very sensitive about how they parent, to do it the right way. They all tend to feel very strongly about the way that they do it is the right way. So if you talk about your way of doing it, which is different, people can feel like you are thereby criticizing what they're doing. So at least from my perspective, I don't want to appear like I was passing judgment on somebody else for being different. At the same time, I don't want, you know, to be criticized for what I was doing.

These women found that speaking about their choices meant that they would encounter judgment or criticism. They chose to silence themselves because they did not like conflict, they did not want to be seen as "educating" people about the benefits of making those types of choices, or because they did not want to impose their views on others.

Final Words About the Experience of Resistance

The experience of mothering for women who believe they are

actively resisting the discourse is complex. It is rewarding while at the same time challenging. The women who participated in this study derived satisfaction from the conviction that their choices were based on thorough thought and consideration. They were convinced that their needs were as important as their children's but found that meeting their needs was not always a simple endeavour. It took ideological work, involving others (preferably loving and invested adults), and juggling to meet their needs. They felt that they had to make certain choices to care for themselves while making sure their children were loved and nurtured.

What does all this mean? It means that resistance is hard work and it takes questioning the messages and expectations placed on mothers. We see these messages of the dominant discourse of motherhood in the cashier's isle on a magazine cover: "Mother's blamed for their daughter's anorexia," "Quality time with your children is essential to their mental health," "Taking care of your growing baby, the do's and don'ts," and so on (Horwitz and Long, 2005). Mothers read the information in the many parenting books. *Oprah, Dr. Phil, Good Morning America, Canada* AM, they all have touched on the topic of parenting and how to mother. The ideology is so powerful that few stop to question it. Few stop to examine the impact it has on mothers.

The women I met and interviewed were consciously navigating through the maze of motherhood. They questioned what society expected of them, and by drawing on other societal discourses and identities they were able to resist and feel empowered. In order to get a full picture of the process of resistance, I explored various factors that were part of this process and that facilitated these women's resistance. I found that certain societal discourses and identities (or subject positions), as well various personal and structural factors created the fabric under which they were able to resist. The following chapter discusses these factors at length.

Chapter 5

Mix and Match:
Discourses, Identities and the
Dominant Discourse of Motherhood

*We are allowed a choice in our own prescription. It is a
basic right of every human being.*
— Virginia Wolf's words, *The Hours*

THIS BOOK IS ABOUT HOW mothers resist the dominant discourse
of motherhood and how they experience resistance. In this
book, I also explore the factors that facilitate resistance and various aspects surrounding the process of resistance. For example, I
discovered that the women I interviewed drew on certain specific
social discourses and identities to construct their own views of
mothering and maternal practices. In addition, all these mothers conformed to different aspects of the dominant discourse of
motherhood. Finally, I explored the personal and social factors
that create a container that supports and facilitates the ability to
resist the discourse. This chapter focuses on my findings of these
factors. To locate these findings, I begin the chapter with a discussion about agency and resistance and the ways they are constrained
by social structures and discourses.

The women in the study identified resistance as empowering.
They felt empowered by their choice to question and resist the
dominant discourse of motherhood. By drawing on alternative
discourses and identifying themselves with certain social identities, these women exercised agency in their own lives. The most
basic definition of agency is the capacity to act (Charrad, 2010).
Therefore, when women are able to act, they exercise some agency.
However, our capacity to act can only be understood within the

constraint of certain social structures specific to each society, including social institutions, groups, culture, and discourses. Emirbayer and Mische offer another definition of agency: the capacity of individuals to "critically shape their own responsiveness to problematic situations" (1998, p. 971). The women whose stories are contained within this book all expressed feeling empowered by critically evaluating social expectations and making their own choices. They exercised agency by resisting a discourse they found oppressive and unfair.

Resistance, empowerment, and agency are all aimed at navigating social systems that may be oppressive or disempowering. However, to understand the complexities of agency and resistance, one must take into account that women's choices are not limitless (Day, Johnson, Milnes and Rickett, 2010). Rather, social structures of power and social discourses create restrictions within which women can resist and construct their own views and practices of mothering (Wetherell, 1995). Whereas agency allows women the capacity to initiate change or transform their lives, it is always limited by the socio-political contexts within which it occurs. Charrad (2010) makes an excellent point when she says, "Agency by definition includes inevitable ambiguity, since it is context-specific and involves contradictory aspects that cannot easily be disentangled" (p. 519). She goes on to explain that women's agentic actions sometimes may only allow "adjustment" to their subordination rather than actual empowering agency that changes their situations radically. In other words, women's resistance may not increase a woman's "real" power but may allow her to navigate a disempowering situation from which she is unable to escape.

Some of the women in my study, such as Astrid and Alice, engaged in acts that they considered resistant but that did not free them from the oppression of intensive mothering. What is interesting is that even though their situations were still experienced as demanding and intense, they felt empowered nevertheless. What this suggests is that empowerment and agency are not straightforward, clear paths.

Bespinar (2010) explains that "Women's empowerment is a multi-dimensional issue that is located at the intersection of constraints and possibilities..." (p.524). In other words, agency and empowerment work within certain constraints where women may conform to some aspects of the dominant discourse while resisting other aspects of it. So, it would be too simplistic to contend that conformity and resistance/empowerment are polarized and discrete (Day et al., 2010). In other words, there is ambiguity within resistance wherein one may be resisting one facet of a discourse while complying with another. Women who resist do so within the limitation of existing rules (Day et al., 2010). Atasoy (2006; as cited in Charrad, 2010) says it well: "Agency assumes that women are active, rational subjects who desire autonomy and self-realization by struggling against the dominant norms and institutions that oppress them" (p. 519). But this assumption, as Atasoy contends, does not take into account that women also actively draw from dominant discourses and norms that constrain their options.

This is a useful way to explain why some women in this study, such as Astrid and Alice, in many ways appeared to be practicing intensive mothering while also resisting; their resistance was constrained by current social structures and practices. For example, Astrid explained that the problem was not that she was practicing Attachment Parenting, but that societal individualistic structures prevented her from parenting this way within community. She was drawing from the dominant discourse in that it suggests that mothers should be closely attached to their children by using Attachment Parenting as her model. On the other hand, she was resisting individualistic discourses that promote independence in children too soon. Although her experience was one of empowerment, she still felt oppressed and marginalized. Charrad (2010) concludes, "Agents support the existing structures, [and also] are both limited and empowered by them, and can create and reshape them" (p. 520). In other words, exercising agency is not a black and white process; rather, it is laden with contradictions that involve resistance and conformity. Agency can affect change but also reproduce the structures it attempts to resist.

Furthermore, resistance is also constrained by the discourses available at any given time (Emirbayer and Mische, 1998). The women in the study resisted and conformed in different ways and to different degrees by drawing on both alternative and dominant discourses. Agency is possible when people navigate within a web of discourses that allow them to reject some and choose others (Foucault, 1978). It is in drawing from alternative, multiple discourses and exercising agency that mothers are able to resist (Day et al., 2010). Discourses create a critical site for active resistance to gender ideologies. Although discourses create this site for resistance, they also create the constraints that limit resistance and open the door to conformity.

Agency is also possible because people are able to choose from various social identities, which are relative to the types of social ideologies, discourses, and the times within which people live (Cochran, 1985; Davies and Harré, 1990). For example, social identities include the good mother, daughter, feminist, good worker, successful woman, or good wife. An individual's ability to actualize her or his desires, dreams, hopes, and values is influenced by the various cultural definitions and descriptions that are available in certain sociocultural settings, and at different historical times.

Discourses interact with a mother's situation, practices, and relations in a manner that has produced specific effects for them at different points in history and time (Cooper, 1994). It is the combination of these factors that allows individuals to exercise a certain degree of agency. In the following pages, I describe various discourses and social identities, explore the ways these mothers conformed to the discourse, and describe the factors that facilitated their resistance.

Alternative Discourses

As part of the analysis of the interviews, I identified a series of possible discourses from which the women may have been drawing. The purpose was to identify the current discourses that appear to be most influential of their experiences of mothering and resistance to the dominant discourse of motherhood. The findings suggest that the process of resistance is complex in that it involves drawing on both alternative and dominant discourses of motherhood. It is important to remember that various discourses interact with one another and often in contradictory ways. This part of the analysis revealed that not only did these women resist the dominant discourse of motherhood but also conformed to it. This is critical because it suggests that mothers resist to different degrees by drawing on a variety of discourses and that it is very difficult to exist completely outside of current dominant discourses. The following remaining sections help to illustrate the many discourses present in these women's narratives.

The various discourses I identified in the women's stories include the discourses of feminism, achievement, individualism, self-care, collectivity, science/expert, attachment/Attachment Parenting, and alternative medicine. I present these in order of significance based on the number of women who ascribed to them. Finally, I present each discourse independent from others despite the interactions between them. It is important to note that these women did not clearly state that they were drawing from these discourses, rather, the analysis yielded these as *possible* discourses from which they may have been drawing. For example, although the discourse of feminism appeared to be central to these women, not all of them considered themselves feminist. I suspect that because the discourse of feminism is now so prevalent in society, it has influenced most women to different degrees.

Feminist discourse

All women appeared to be drawing (overtly or covertly) from various aspects of the feminist discourse. In this section, I will briefly mention some aspects of feminist discourses to locate the findings of my study. It is not intended as an in-depth review of feminist theory. Feminist theories and philosophies are diverse but they share some common characteristics (Ramazanoglu, 1989). For example, all versions of feminist thought maintain that the current state of the relationship between men and women where women are subordinated to men is unsatisfactory and must be changed (Greer, 1972; Ramazanoglu, 1989; Weedon, 1997). Most feminists agree that feminism aims to change society and transform male/female relationships so that all people can have the opportunity to fulfill their human potential. Furthermore, many forms of feminism reflect principles that are intended for political practice (Rich, 1986; Weedon, 1997).

Feminist thought also strives to break down the barriers that prevent women from having control over their lives. Feminist writings on motherhood have also promoted equality for women in the home, noted that current ideologies and norms are oppressive and disempowering to women, and called for change and resistance (Douglas and Michaels, 2004; Green, 2005; Gordon, 1990; Greer, 1972; Hays, 1996; Porter, 2010; O'Reilly, 2004; Rich, 1986). They have also encouraged analyses of power differentials that disadvantage mothers in order to create more equitable social structures (Kinser, 2008, 2010). Feminist theorists have also aimed to change the redistribution of social power so that women are able to exercise authority, access resources, and have the social status that will create opportunities for experiencing self-determination (Kinser, 2010).

The women in this study all appeared to be drawing on some aspect of feminist discourse. Some explicitly identified their thoughts as being feminist. Carla, for example, said, "For some reason, I've turned out with really strong feminist beliefs." Carla had chosen to relinquish the primary caregiver role to her partner in order to pursue her interests. She explained that she never imagined herself having to take on that primary role. She felt that this way of thinking was clearly informed by her feminist beliefs. Astrid was another participant who identified herself as a feminist:

> *My beliefs about feminism are that part of being a woman, and that the struggle against patriarchy is the struggle of caregiving and children. Because that's what women have done historically, and will continue to do because we have babies (laughs). And ah ... and on the other hand ... that's ... the inclusive part about feminism. But on the other hand, all those other things that feminism is about, you know, being a human being, and not being the doormat, and not completely losing yourself to your kids.*

Astrid draws on feminist thought in order to explain her position as a mother, woman, and human being to elucidate that she does not see herself as a doormat just because she stays home.

Some women emphasized that the rights of all human beings need to be honoured. Their feminist views were clearly in support of the idea that all human rights are worthy of respect. This influenced their resistance by confirming to them that they, as mothers and human beings, have rights too. Their desire to balance meeting their children's needs as well as their own was also influenced by their belief that all human beings have the right to be respected and have their needs met. Louise, for example, explained in her interview, "I don't consider myself only a feminist but a humanist. I believe that all human beings deserve respect."

Some women also believed that they should not restrict themselves to only their own private lives, but rather to be involved in the public sphere as activists for women and children. For example, Lilith explained that she is an activist for social justice:

> *But I'm also a person for social justice and social fairness.... I've always have had very deep beliefs in social justice, and everybody being equal and everybody having the right to opportunities and stuff like that.*

In analyzing these women's interviews, I found that all of them were drawing on some aspect of the feminist discourse. They were against the idea that mothers should sacrifice their needs all the time and strongly believed that mothers have rights. They believed that women are human beings and as such should have their rights respected. Many of the women also adhered to the discourse of achievement—fought for by feminists—so that women can access opportunities.

Discourse of achievement

Many of the women explicitly or implicitly appeared to draw on the discourse of self-achievement and self-actualization. This discourse is quite widespread in countries like Canada and the United States. Maslow's hierarchy of needs is an example of a theory that describes self-actualization and the reaching of one's potential as one of our primary needs (Heathernigton and Park, 1986). Maslow's theory posits that when human beings have their basic needs of food, shelter, safety, and love met, they are then in a position to reach the need to self-actualize and their full potential. The theory suggests that self-actualization is important to being healthy and whole. The idea that personal achievements and productivity contribute to a person's self-esteem is common. In our society, being productive is often linked to reaching one's potential and having worth.

Related to the individualistic, materialistic, and capitalist structures of the United States and Canada (Kim, Triandis, Kagitcibasi, Choi, and Yoon, 1994), the discourse of achievement promotes the pursuit of dreams and having the right to do so (Kofodimos, 1993; Rountree, 2000). Rountree reports that 30-something women today tend to have high expectations of achieving successful careers and raising children. Many of the women I interviewed experienced similar desires and expectations. They resisted the dominant discourse of motherhood by being convinced that they have a right to pursue their interests and to meet their own needs. Holding this belief supported them in achieving in areas or activities they considered important because, contrary to what the dominant discourse of motherhood promotes, they did not believe they had to be the 'ever-present mother'. For example, Catherine, who wanted to spend time with her daughter and had chosen to pursue her career, mentioned that she was planning to go to law school in the near future. For other women, achievement was not as important. They spoke of "interests," rather than careers, and of contributing or giving back. Again, this illustrates how resistance and mothering is comprised of a complexity of practices, discourses, and choices. Different women drew, to varying degrees, on the discourses available to them. Furthermore, it is important to note that the discourse of achievement appears to be in opposition to the dominant discourse of motherhood in that it does not promote selflessness (Hays, 1996).

Individualism

The women who were interviewed belonged mostly to white, middle-class Canadian society, which for the most part is an individualistic one. Most of them appeared to be drawing on the discourse of individualism in one way or another. This discourse promotes the idea that people should be independent, self-sufficient, and self-realized (Myers, 2000). It is associated with attitudes such as "doing it my way," I will do "what works for me," I need to "question authority," and I will "do my own thing." By drawing on the discourse of individualism, these women believed that they had a right to be independent and that their children would benefit from learning to be independent as well. This discourse was apparent in their resistance in relation to the following: (a) independent children are comfortable when they are left in the care of others; (b) viewing their children as independent people freed the women to pursue what matters to them; and (c) independence gives people the freedom to question societal discourses and expectations and make their own choices.

The women believed that they had a right to make choices that "worked for them" and their families. This type of statement is consistent with the individualistic mentality of doing what is "best for me" (Myers, 2000). Some women spoke about independence and taking care of themselves as being important which contradicts the promotion of sacrifice on the part of mothers within the dominant discourse of motherhood. Other women spoke about how having independent children supported their resistance because it allowed them to seek other activities and interests away from them. For example, Lilith explained that she stayed at home with her daughters for a year and a half but that as soon as they appeared to be more independent and able to socialize with others, she decided to leave them at daycare in order to pursue a career exploration course and later an education: "And at a year and a half, I figured they are pretty independent, they like to do stuff, they are pretty independent to go and socialize, you know. That way I can go and do something better."

For most of the women being individuals with unique interests and a right to those interests was important. This particular view was in contrast to the dominant discourse that promotes the idea that mothers should be ever-present and sacrificial. However, some women struggled because they believed that everyone has rights but that for mothers to claim those rights, either their children, family life, or health had to be compromised. For example, Astrid and Lisa were not willing to sacrifice time with their children in order to achieve their goals. This choice resulted in a process of intensive mothering. They both saw this inescapable fact as a failure of society to be more communal and supportive of mothers rather than as a failure on their part to be more independent and less sacrificial. Individualistic discourse has influenced the belief that each person is responsible for his or her own well-being, that individuals should be self-reliant and, therefore, in charge of their own self-care (Myers, 2000). These women's experiences were influenced by this individualistic discourse. They resisted the dominant discourse of motherhood by claiming that they have a right to meet their needs while also holding that they are the ones responsible to meet them. Whereas some of them believed that there are aspects of mothering that could be shared with others or communally, their resistance was often a solitary endeavor.

Self-care

The discourse of self-care is quite prominent today. It promotes the idea that we must take care of our physical and mental health by engaging in healthy eating, exercise, leisure, and healthy relationships. Most women spoke about the importance of taking care of themselves. This discourse is closely related to individualistic discourse in that it promotes individual responsibility for people's psychological, mental, and physical health (Horwitz and Long, 2005; Pollock, 1988). Collectivist discourse, in contrast, promotes collective responsibility for the health of its members (Kim et al., 1994; Myers, 2000). The women who participated in this study endeavored to take care of their health by exercising, athletics, taking breaks from their children, traveling, reading, talking to friends, doing yoga, taking care of their needs, and keeping a balance between mothering and other activities, work, or interests. Catherine emphasized that it was extremely important for her to take care of herself so that she could feel well. She explained that this made her whole and happy. It was important for her to take care of her physical, mental, and emotional well-being. Many of the women believed that it was important to take care of themselves because they had a right to do so. Being healthy would then allow them to perform all their various roles better. Jane's said:

> I wanted to make sure that I was looking after myself as I was raising my children. It was very important for me to have children, but I also knew that if I didn't recharge

*over the years, I did not want to turn into this burnt out
person, and be resentful and angry.*

In sum, by drawing on the discourse of self-care, the women
resisted the idea that mothers should forget their needs in order to
take care of the needs of their children. Whereas taking responsibility
for their own self-care and the pursuit of their interests was necessary, some of the women also valued community and collectivity
as desirable resources for women who are raising children.

Collectivity

Most of the women I interviewed believed in the value of community. Many explicitly voiced their belief that a mother needs a
community around her if she is going to make space for herself.
Contrary to the discourse of individualism, the discourse of collectivism is characterized by cooperation, collaboration, and in-
terdependence rather than independence (Kim et al., 1994; Myers,
2000). To different degrees, the women in this study described
how community and friends could be very important for women
during their mothering years. Many of the women felt that community support can free mothers from having to be ever-present,
sacrificial, and overwhelmed with the sole responsibility for their
children. Drawing on this discourse supported their resistance by
influencing their views about mothers and the degree to which presence and responsibility were important. Some of the women were
active in pursuing community for themselves and their families.
Others, such as Astrid and Lisa, had a very limited community and
yearned for more people to connect with; they both felt isolated
and with limited support systems. In both cases, their families
lived far away and they did not have that many close friends on
which they could rely.

Kate and Louise explained that they had been successful at
building strong community supports around them. This relieved
them of the practice of intensive mothering. For others, the idea
of community was different. Anna, for example, believed that it
was important for her to develop a community of support with
daycare providers and extended family when they were available.
Many mothers find themselves isolated in their motherwork. Build-

ing a community that mothers can trust is challenging, but based on the statements of the women in this study, it may be a key factor in being able to resist. In conclusion, the majority of these women saw the value of community as a way to avoid isolation and mothering alone. They rejected the facets of the discourse that suggest that mothers are the best caregivers and the only ones who can raise children.

It is important to note how the collectivity discourse stands in opposition to the individualistic discourse, which, as mentioned earlier, was also important to them. Discourses are usually made up of a series of tenets. When people resist, they may resist some aspects but not others. These women wove their own constructions of mothering and maternal practice by drawing from specific tenets in various discourses. In this way, each of them was able to draw from the discourses even when they appear to be contradictory to one another.

Science/expert discourse

Most of the women I interviewed talked about how they consulted "scientific" or "expert" literature in order to assist their decision-making process, make sense of issues they have encountered, or learn parenting strategies. The science/expert discourse promotes the idea that science has the right answers to guide our understanding and knowledge of our families and ourselves (Arnup, 1994; Douglas and Michaels, 2004; Hays, 1996). This discourse was influential both to the women's resistance but also to their conformity to the dominant discourse of motherhood. They resisted by seeking information that supported them in challenging some of the myths associated with the dominant discourse of motherhood.

Many of the women in the study explained that reading books was helpful in guiding some of their mothering. Accepting the tenets of baby books generally contributed to conforming to the dominant discourse of motherhood. Carla explained: "I follow most of the things in the baby books. I take her to a regular family doctor, give immunizations, feed her what you're supposed to, and all those things." However, many sought answers to their experience as mothers. They found the initial experience difficult and confusing and this led them to read material on topics such as motherhood and feminism. This became highly influential to their resistance of the dominant discourse of motherhood. They found that reading feminist literature freed them to perceive their experience as normal rather than deviant. Nancy described how she read a book that was very helpful towards normalizing her experience:

> *There was a book that I read in those first few months. It's a novel; it's called* The Mother Knot. *But I remember reading that book, and thinking, "thank God!" And it was a book about this woman's mothering experience, and it was very much about how she had wanted to have the kid whatever, and yet, what it did to her to have the kids. And ultimately how she resolved it. And just seeing that in black and white, I knew that whatever the dominant ideas out there, there was at least one other person who had the courage to write about this. So that meant that there were many others. And like everybody, I was going to do what was right for me. Ah ... it was a very powerful book.*

Some women emphasized that they consulted the literature when they were faced with challenges or decisions that were difficult to handle. This is consistent with the dominant discourse of motherhood in that it encourages mothers to be well informed and to consult experts for answers to their questions. For example, Theo explained that she engaged in 'researching' information about home births in order to make sense of the many options that were available to her: "But we did the research, we did all the reading, and we discovered it was perfectly safe. And we felt really confident with our decision." In sum, many of the women consulted various sources of expert information for various reasons. This practice appears to be common whenever people encounter difficulties, are curious, or motivated to learn (Arnup, 1994; Thurer, 1994). The women sought expert knowledge, in part as conformity to the dominant discourse of motherhood, and in part as support for their resistance.

Attachment/Attachment Parenting

Every single mother I interviewed expressed that they loved their children deeply and were committed to their well-being. This experience may be influenced by our current discourse on attachment and love toward our children (Ainsworth, Blehar, Waters and Wall, 1978; Bowlby, 1991; Thurer, 1996). The degrees to which these women drew from this discourse varied.

Jane expressed her love for her children in the following words:

> To know that this person is someone that my husband and I created, I love him to bits, I'm going to love my child. That was one of the things that the midwife said, when Mary was about to be born, she said, you know, just love them and everything else kind of falls into place. That really hits home for me a lot of the time. I just keep thinking I am just going to love them.

Others were committed to the practice of Attachment Parenting. Consistent with this perspective, Aibrean explained that she sleeps with her baby: "We sleep together, not because I don't like it, I like it. I've talked to parents who don't like it, but do it because it's, you know, the whole sacrifice thing. I sleep fine. I sleep wonderfully." These examples illustrate how these women have drawn on the discourse of love and attachment in order to practice mothering in this manner. This discourse manifested itself as an important factor in the process of juggling and balancing between their needs and their children's. Their love for their children was central in how they spoke about their children and how they wanted to mother them. If we suspend a judgmental eye, given that many readers may be thinking that practicing Attachment Parenting is a strong example of intensive mothering and we are open to the many ways that mothers can choose to care for their children, we may be able to appreciate Astrid's attitude: "It is not Attachment Parenting or staying at home that is the problem, it is a patriarchal, individualistic system that does not support mothers or provide community for them that is the problem."

Discourse of alternative medicine

Finally, many of the women adhered to the discourse of alternative medicine and consequently believe that the mainstream medical model of birth and baby care is not always the best for their children and their families. This discourse encourages people to challenge mainstream medical practices in order to make informed, and what is construed as more "natural," choices (Arnup, 1994). Many of these women did not vaccinate their children, they gave birth at home, practiced extended breastfeeding, and ate organic food or had a vegetarian diet. Alice, for example, gave birth to her children at home and chose not to vaccinate them. She explained how in making these choices she encountered much criticism and many pressures from others to do it "right." She explained, as did the others who engaged in these practices, that making these decisions was not easy. She read and researched the topics extensively. Madelaine felt similarly:

> *I decided not to vaccinate. And that's also something where you're going against the medical model, which says that that's the right thing to do. It is your responsibility not only to your own child, but to the community because you're protecting, you know, you're building community immunity to something. And after the first three immunizations I decided to stop because of all this information I read.*

Adhering to the discourse of alternative health may also be an aspect of their feminist views and resistance of mainstream expectations about how mothers should care for their children. For many years, feminists have argued against medical experts taking control over how women give birth or how they care for their infants (Arnup, 1994).

Final Comments on Discourses

My in-depth analysis of the 15 women's stories yielded a complex web of factors, discourses, and experiences that suggest that we cannot divide mothers into two groups: those who resist and those who don't. It would be more appropriate to say that women resist to different degrees and in different ways and that some women may resist very little or may question very little. In those cases, raising consciousness may support an empowering experience of motherhood for them. My analysis of the interviews was useful, not only because it identified how these women resisted and what their experiences of resistance were, but also because it reveals that resistance is not a simple, clear-cut process; it is laden with complexities, unique individual choices, a range of influences, and various degrees of ideological work. Through my detailed analysis, I was also able to identify a series of social identities to which each of the women ascribed. These identities were intertwined within the discourses from which the women drew. Examining these social identities may also shed some light into how social discourses impact our practices and the way we see ourselves.

Social Identities

Social identities, or "subject positions," refer to identities that are connected to various ideologies and discourses in society (Little, 1999). It is through these identities that people are able to exercise choice in relation to the discourses to which they adhere (Davies and Harré, 1990). The particular images, metaphors, story lines, and concepts through which a person relates to the world are contained in those identities, and are directly related to practices that are driven by various discourses. These identities, along with the discourses I have identified, are part of a container of sorts wherein the women's experiences and meanings thrived. In order to reveal how the women situated themselves in their societal context, I identified five social identities to which they adhered: caring, responsible mother; independent woman/individual; educated/professional; critical thinker; and, activist. As a result of my analysis of the women's stories, I discuss social identities in order of significance based on the number of women I located within that identity.

Caring, responsible mother

All these women saw themselves as caring and responsible mothers. This social identity is influenced by the dominant discourse of motherhood. Mothers may not have identified themselves in the same manner at other times in history or even in modern times in other cultures. For example, in colonial America, a father was expected to be the main influence on and responsible presence in his child's life (Albanese, 2010; Thurer, 1994). In current times, mothers are expected to take on the main role or to view themselves as responsible (Douglas and Michaels, 2004; Hay, 1996; Thurer, 1994). This discourse also interacts with the discourse of individualism, which has resulted in families acting as independent units where the mother is expected to take the main responsibility for children.

The way that being a caring, responsible mother was manifest in the lives of these women varied based on their views and practices of mothering. For example, some women believed that pursuing their interests and meeting their needs made them a good mother. In this manner they viewed themselves as being caring and responsible mothers. In addition, all of these women felt satisfied with how they mothered their children. They felt they were doing a good job. As an illustration of caring as a mother, Jane said:

> *But I think, overall, I feel like I'm a pretty good mother. They are loved, they're being clothed and fed to the best of our ability right now. And quite often that's how I feel.*

Like many of the other women, Jane felt intense love for her children. Others, like Louise, also expressed their sense of responsibility and interest in their children, "My job as a mom is a job that has to be done, and it's one that I love, I love it. It's a big part of me." These women's stories revealed that they took their role as mothers very seriously. They often carefully considered the options before them so that their decisions would have positive impacts for their children. These examples illustrate their sense of commitment to doing what they thought was best for their children. Their commitment to this social identity illustrates that resistance occurs in conjunction with other factors and discourses. Some of their views are consistent with those of the dominant discourse of motherhood: the image of the caring, loving mother has been identified by some historians and academics as a phenomenon of modern times and not an absolute truth for mothers throughout history (Hays, 1996; Thurer, 1994).

Independent woman/individual

Interestingly, all these mothers appeared to identify themselves as independent women. This social identity is possibly influenced by feminist and individualistic discourses, which are very significant in our present historical period in the West. These discourses promote the idea that women have a right to pursue careers, to be financially independent, and to "be all that [they] can be" (Douglas and Michaels, 2004; Myers, 2000). The women in this study adhered to this social identity to different degrees. Carla and Catherine, for example, relinquished the main caregiver role to their partners in order to pursue their careers. Some of Catherine's statements illustrate this point: "And I don't know, I think I didn't want to be ever in a position where I was dependent upon anyone." She remained very interested in participating in her child's life but didn't need to be present all the time. At times, this created some frustration in balancing concurrent demands to be at work and with her child.

Being an independent woman did not always mean pursuing a career for the women in the study. For some of the women being independent meant that they had rights to pursue other interests that mattered to them, or to be independent thinkers. Astrid, for example, was not pursuing a career, but explored feminist thought by reading and researching the topic. She is an artist, considers herself a social activist, and is involved in various non-profit groups as a volunteer. Many of the mothers believed in their rights as human beings to have their needs met and to pursue their interests because they deserved it, not because this would benefit their children. In sum, the women's identity as independent women supported their resistance because it freed them to have their own independent beliefs, and to claim that as independent women they have rights to make their own choices and decisions.

Educated/professional

Some of the women had identities that included being educated and being a professional. Even though most of the women had some post-secondary education, not all of them appeared to claim this factor as an identity. Those who did, spoke at length about how their education or professional interests were an important aspect of their lives. They were committed to their careers or education even though they encountered some tension in carrying out their professional/educational endeavours because of the demands of mothering. For example, Carla went back to work two weeks after giving birth to her daughter. She explained how this was useful in maintaining her identity:

> *You almost lose all sense of identity for a brief period. I think a lot of people that I've spoken to have found that too. And work is kind of something you can cling to. You go to work; your baby's not there, and apart from any physical things that are still going on, you are yourself again.*

Carla was not alone. Other women found that being with their young infants was not sufficient in their lives. They resisted because they did not feel completely fulfilled by their roles as mothers and found that their professional lives granted them other rewards like feeling competent or challenged. Other women like Louise and Aibrean, for example, had completed post-secondary degrees but during the interview they did not emphasize this aspect of their lives as being particularly significant.

Independent, critical thinker

The women I interviewed seemed to see themselves as active thinkers who were free to question societal messages and ide-ologies. They appeared to see themselves as independent, critical thinkers. These women described themselves as often questioning the status quo. Some of them remembered themselves questioning social expectations even as young children. Lilith, for example, described how when she was a young girl she always challenged the way adults behaved. She has continued to question most of what is expected from her:

> *I mean, I've always challenged the status quo. And I think that it's also because of my own life experiences. I think*

that a lot of my parenting has to do with the fact that I don't follow the status quo and stuff. So if I'm not follow-ing the status quo, I don't follow the status quo parenting styles either. There's a lot of people now who were raised by moms from the '60s and stuff. So I don't see how I can possibly screw up my kids badly, from this lifestyle, you know. I mean, 'cause, like I love this nature/nurture debate stuff.

Aibrean defined herself as a "questioner" and explained that she questioned many norms that she observed as a young child and has continued to be that way in her adult life.

But I remember, or maybe I've just been a questioner. I remember a woman at our church, she breastfed her son until he was four or five, and she just did it wherever. I remember my church being, 'Oh, my God, that's so hor-rible! Horrifying, why would she do that?' And I thought, why does she do that? Not, Oh my Gosh it's horrible, or my Gosh it's good. Why does she do that? So I think I've always just been a questioner. And I've always looked at things, but I've always saw that this is the way it's sup-posed to be, that this is what you're supposed to do, and I've always said, why? Nobody taught me to do that.

In sum, all of the women saw themselves as critical thinkers of mainstream expectations on mothering as part of their process of resistance.

Activist

Some of these mothers identified themselves as activists. This social identity is related to feminist discourses that encourage women to become active in the political realm by speaking up against women's oppression. This is evident in a main credence of feminism, that the personal is political (Ramazanoglu, 1989). Jane's story illustrates the commitment to activism. Jane completed her master's degree thesis on the topic of extended breastfeeding because she wanted to contribute to mothers by normalizing this practice. In a similar vein, Lilith joined demonstrations to protest for the rights of single mothers in British Columbia. Finally, Madelaine was involved in the movement to encourage politicians and members of society to acknowledge mothers' contributions as work while struggling to make sense of her own work as a mother:

> *And I was doing policy research, so all my work through this time was around writing and researching, mostly on unpaid work, which was the biggest area. I would give some talks about it and I would do this while I was living the experience of being the mother at home.*

Astrid clearly defined herself as an activist "for women, children and youth." For these women being actively involved in making a difference in the lives of mothers and trying to change the world was very important.

Concluding Comments to Social Identities

It is interesting to see how women who resist view themselves. People draw from current social discourses and definitions to explain how they see themselves and these women were no exception. They positioned themselves within currently available cultural definitions. And what is most interesting is that although they resisted aspects of the discourse, they also conformed in some ways. They were all invested in being good mothers, which is a central tenet of the dominant discourse of motherhood. This suggests that resistance is not black and white; it is not all resistance or all conformity. In the case of these mothers, some of their identities were consistent with their resistance to the discourse. On the other hand, some of these identities—such as being a caring, responsible mother—were related to mainstream identities for mothers. The types of identities they claimed illustrate the interplay of dominant and alternative discourses in their experiences and practices. When I began the study, we knew little about the process of resistance in this context. I was surprised by how intricate and complex resistance is. Women who choose to resist the discourse are challenged to navigate between dominant and alternative discourses and none of the women in my study lived completely outside the dominant discourse of motherhood. Their resistance, identities, experiences, and choices varied significantly. Given that they all navigated a web of discourses, and in every case they resisted but also conformed to the discourse, I analyzed their stories to identify how they conformed. The following section describes my findings.

Instances of Conformity

When I began my study, I naively thought that resistance would look like a radical departure from the way the compliant mother mothered. As I interviewed the women and delved into an in-depth analysis of their stories, I began to see that my original assumptions were far from the reality of these women. Yes, they resisted: they were aware of the social pressures and expectations; they questioned; they modified their practices and departed from some of the social expectations contained in the discourse. But they also conformed to the same discourse they were resisting. So, in analyzing the interviews, I looked for instances in which they were influenced by the dominant discourse of motherhood. The instances of conformity that I identified in these women's stories included: (a) mothers should be present; (b) mothers should be role models, best caregivers, calm, good mothers, and influential; (c) strong attachments and love are essential for children; (d) expert advice is valuable; (e) daycare is not the best option for children; and, (f) children are fragile and can be damaged. The findings in this section illustrate how the process of resistance is complex and multifaceted.

Mothers should be present

All the women I interviewed believed that it was important for them to spend time with their children, to be present and to not be away from them for prolonged periods of time. The degree to which each of them believed this tenet varied. For example, women like Alice and Astrid acted more fully on this belief in that they chose to stay home and be the primary caregivers of their children. Astrid, who identified as a feminist, explained that she wants to be around her children as much as possible:

I feel that I must make it clear that I certainly do not condemn women who choose to work outside the home. There can be no doubt that she is entitled to that choice. And nor can I blame her for doing so. I certainly understand the need to do something else. I do believe, however, that she compromises a lot to do so, including her kids' interests and her own. She deprives her kids and herself of precious time together. Again I reiterate that she is not to blame for this impossible choice, it is only patriarchy. The question is not whether women should do work outside of caregiving; she must. But rather, how will that work be accomplished in relation to her caregiving responsibilities.

Several of the women explained that, while they needed and wanted to be away from their children because it was important for them to pursue their own interests and to have time to themselves, being away for too long was not acceptable. Jane's story illustrates this point well. She explained that she did not want to be home with her children all the time, but that she did not want to be away for too many hours either, and she therefore sought to balance the two competing needs. Furthermore, she believed that a parent must "be there" for her children rather than have a paid caregiver to take care of them:

I don't want to be away from my children for eight, never mind twelve, hours; it is pretty well impossible when you're breast-feeding. (laughs) ... I find that when I am all in one or all in the other, I am just not happy. It drives me smoothly mad, actually. There was a time when my daughter was in daycare. It was only a couple of days a week, but it just drove me mad that I was unable to be there for her.

Like many of the women in the study, Jane struggled to balance her time with, and away from, her children. She reconciled some of this struggle by having her husband stay home with the children while she was away. Jane resisted the discourse by relinquishing the main caregiving role to her husband, but conformed with the discourse by believing that she should not be away from her children for too long. This is a good example of how resistance is not a black and white process.

Most of the other women explained that they believed that an important part of their role as mothers is to participate in their children's lives by being near them. Many assume that this aspect of the discourse is a "truth." Western research has confirmed for them the value of close attachments as being essential to the psychological well-being of children (e.g., Bowlby, 1991; Sears and Sears, 2001). Ignored by adhering to this discursive belief is that in more collective societies, children may not distinguish their biological mother from other "mothers" (Bernard, 1974) or that in some communities, mothering is shared. For example, many African American women in the United States practice *othermothering* by allowing other non-blood friends and neighbors to share in the upbringing of their children (Edwards, 2000).

Individualistic societies have provided mothers with discourses that are consistent with individualistic mothering practices: these, in turn, exclude the involvement of others outside the nuclear family (Contratto, 1984). Rather than seeing children as the responsibility of the community, this responsibility is given solely to the mother and maybe to the father if he is sufficiently present. Some of the women in this study explained that communal mothering would be the ideal but that they are unable to access this type of arrangement within current societal structures. These women believed that involving other loving and responsible caretakers in raising their children would significantly alleviate the intensity of their mothering. Still, they found it necessary to be highly present in the lives of their children in order to avoid harming them. An important point is needed here. The fact that a dominant discourse of motherhood is oppressive may not mean that *everything* within that discourse is false or damaging. Attachment may or may not be positive for children; what does become oppressive is the component of fear that accompanies this aspect of the discourse, which would have one believe that if mothers do not provide the right amount of attachment, their children will be damaged.

Mother as role model, best caregiver, calm, good mother, and influential

All the mothers I interviewed subscribed to these aspects of the dominant discourse of motherhood. The discourse promotes an image of mothers as 'special' in their children's lives; mothers are expected to always be calm, patient, and kind, to provide the best care, and to be an important role model for their children (Thurer, 1994). Most of the women I interviewed saw themselves as role models for their children, and therefore believed they had a duty to behave and act in a manner that would be a positive example for their children.

Louise, for example, believed that children should learn to be independent and respectful, pursue their interests, and reach their full potential. Given that her children were interested in athletics, she said, "Well, I am a bit of a role model, because they are also athletes, so, ah...I've had a lot of personal success, they see a lot of trophies and medals in the back there." By conducting herself as an independent woman who pursued athletics and graduate school, Louise felt she was modeling independence and the possibility of being champion athletes to her daughters. Catherine also explained how she saw herself as a role model who should set an example for her daughter:

> *My role…. I think the biggest part of it had been just role modeling. I talk to Alysia about how her grandmother worked with me, and how she parented me, and how she was home all the time. And you know, she'll sometimes ask, 'How come you don't do that?' We always have talked about it. So I think, probably the biggest thing is just setting an example for her.*

By holding these beliefs, these women accepted individualistic discourses that place mothers as unique forces that must behave well at all times, and therefore are very important influences in their children's development. This way of thinking places strong pressures on mothers to be perfect, and therefore experience feelings of guilt when they depart from this expectation. The women I interviewed did not expect themselves to be perfect; they just saw themselves as modeling what they wanted their children to learn, but without the pressure of taking all the responsibility for how their children turned out. More collective societies may not place such burdens on mothers because they more equally share the responsibility for raising children. Some aboriginal people of Australia, for example, involve maternal siblings, grandmothers, and other elders as role models for all children (Huggings and Huggings, 1996). Consequently, their children do not view their biological mothers as the only influence in their lives. Other women are called "aunties" and provide guidance, discipline, love, and attention to several children at once. These children have 'attachments' to many 'aunties' so that even the loss of their biological mother is not experienced in isolation or in fear of loneliness (Huggings and Huggings, 1996). English-speaking North American individualistic and capitalistic ideologies set the stage for mothers to hold the burden of being models and guides for their children. Mothers may have no alternative but to take on these burdens in the absence of a collective of maternal/paternal figures and other structural supports.

Strong attachments and love are important for children

One very strong influence in the dominant discourse of motherhood is the theory of attachment (Bowlby, 1991; Sears and Sears, 2001). Mothers in our current historical period are led to believe that they must love their children intensely, that this is the natural state of being, and that a mother's love and caretaking of her children is essential to their well being and development (Contratto, 1984; Thurer, 1994). All the mothers in the study expressed that they loved their children. Some of them also used the word "attachment" when describing their beliefs and practices around mothering. For example, Madelaine explained that her children "are the most important thing." Aibrean, on the other hand, explained that she loves her children and this is important but that she "does not have to feel loving all the time." Anna expressed it simply, "I think they need unconditional love, which means, well that's a huge thing."

The mothers' beliefs about attachment also influenced with whom they were willing to leave their children. Many believed that caregivers should only be those with whom the children will develop strong relationships. Astrid felt that children should be taken care of by people who love them, "but there is something to be said for close family and friends who have a long term investment that is not monetary." Similarly, Carla emphasized that having other loving adults take care of her daughter is essential: "I am just one of the caring adults in her life"; she did not, however, believe in taking her to daycare centers.

Expert advice is valuable

One of the core tenets of the discourse is that mothers should consult the advice of experts who have come up with the "right" answers for parents. As I mentioned before, all the women in the study had consulted expert advice at one time or another and in many cases found it helpful. Most of them accessed this advice from written materials. The twentieth century was notable for placing science as the avenue to "facts" and "truth" (Arnup, 1994; Douglas and Michaels, 2004; Thurer, 1994). Medicine and psychology were promoted as holding expert knowledge mothers needed to learn in order to raise their children the "right way." This led mothers to read parenting and other types of books with the hope of finding information that would teach them to mother the correctly. The mothers in this study were no exception. Alice's words illustrate this point: "I have more time than my mom had and more resources than she had, in order to research my choices and stuff like that." Although Anna found that reading baby books was unhelpful when she first became a mother because these were inaccurate in describing her experience, she consulted books later on in search for ideas on how to deal with her preteen daughter.

This aspect of the dominant discourse of motherhood does not allow women to realize that in other historical periods and cultures, wisdom and knowledge has been derived from sources such as elders, intuition, religion, cultural practices, and so on (Badinter, 1981; Mawami, 2001; Thomas, 2000). I do not suggest that consulting experts is "right" or "wrong" but that in our current historical period in the West, we often ignore other sources of knowledge when they have not been "proven" scientifically. Furthermore, it may be important to question 'scientific' findings given that they have often been used as *proof* for some of the very tenets of the dominant discourse of motherhood.

Daycare is not the best option for children

Consistent with the perception that daycare is not the best option for children, some of the mothers in the study avoided taking their children to daycare. The reason for this belief was that daycare workers are not as invested in the children and won't love them as family and friends do. Catherine and Jane, for example, briefly tried to take their respective daughters to daycare and experienced significant guilt. They felt guilty because they believed that children need to be cared for by someone who loves them and is invested in them. Both of them decided that they would find alternative care and, in both cases, their partners took on the role of primary caregivers. This sentiment is evident in Catherine's words:

> And we tried daycare, it didn't work, it wasn't for us. I felt guilty leaving her with someone else. And we came to an agreement that we did not want someone else to raise her.

This is an interesting example of the complexity of resistance; although these two women *resisted* the idea that they had to be the primary caregiver, they conformed to the dominant discourse of motherhood by believing that children can be hurt if they are not cared by relatives or close family friends. Carla also described how the decision to have a child at the time that she made it was largely influenced by knowing that her mother-in-law and sister-in-law were willing to participate in caring for her baby:

> Aaron's mother and sister look after Ellie a lot. And I think that, had they not been around and if we hadn't known that that's the way it would work, we would have waited and not had a child at this time. Because we can't really take her to daycare, and I really didn't want to look after her all the time by myself and be the main person.

Most of the women believed that their children benefit from being cared for by people who love them. What complicates this assumption is that in countries like the United States and Canada, many white, middle-class mothers do not have access to other adults who "love" their children. Two of the women in this study shared parenting with their partners to avoid taking their child to daycare whereas others did not have this option, thereby resulting in more intensive mothering. Furthermore, daycare centers are a way to access collective practices in individualistic societies. These contradictions are complicated by the fact that mothers are told of the "dangers" of daycare centers by faulty media reports. They fear that their children may be sexually abused, or that their children might not be as close to them as they should be, or that daycare might negatively affect their self-esteem (Thurer, 1994). Consistent with these beliefs, the women experienced guilt by leaving their children in the care of strangers because of their lack of trust in others, a widespread element of the culture of fear in the U.S. and Canada (Glassner, 2000).

Children are fragile and can be damaged

Just as there is a dominant discourse of motherhood, there is also a discourse of childhood. All the women appeared to adhere to aspects of the current dominant discourse on children. This discourse promotes a view of children as innocent, fragile, always good, deserving of love regardless of their actions, and needing to have a childhood (Badinter, 1981). The women expressed this in various ways: children need to be loved; children need to be respected; children "need structure"; they "should not be spanked or yelled at"; they need their mothers when they are young; and children are the "most important thing." These are some examples of statements made by the participants that reflect dominant views about children.

In sum, although these women resisted, they also conformed to the dominant discourse of motherhood. Their convictions and values were a combination of alternative and dominant discourses. This begins to paint a picture of the complexity of the process of resistance but it is not yet complete. Many things come together that allow a mother to resist. It is not only her own ideological work, questioning of the discourse, or the types of discourses she draws from but also many other personal factors. In conducting the analysis of their narratives, I was curious about the types of personal and situational factors that supported these mothers in their resistance. In the next chapter I discuss my findings in this area.

Chapter 6

The Container: Social and Personal Factors that Facilitate Resistance

Thousands of candles can be lighted from a single candle, and the life of the candle will not be shortened. Happiness never decreases by being shared.　　　—Buddha

S O FAR I HAVE EXPLORED how these women resisted, how they experienced their resistance, and what discourses and identities influenced their resistance including those related to the dominant discourse of motherhood. But one could ask, what was *unique* to these women that allowed them to engage in a process of resistance? What personal, social, and situational factors supported these women's resistance? Resistance and agency occur within and are supported by certain social structures and factors. The stories of the women I interviewed revealed some of the factors that appeared to facilitate their resistance. These various factors were synthesized in an interaction that created the possibility to resist. Several personal factors were apparent: (a) the mother's own experiences of mothering; (b) the mother's present situation; (c) the mother's early life and past experiences; and, (d) the mother's awareness of social structures.

Resistance is Influenced by the Experience and Practice of Being a Mother

For many of these mothers, their early mothering experiences were, in many cases, the catalyst for resistance. They described their first infant as "difficult," "demanding," "colicky," "crying

153

too much," or "high strung." Because those first experiences were very difficult, these women felt disillusioned because the fairy tale promised by the dominant discourse did not manifest itself. This led them re-evaluate their beliefs about their power to understand, soothe, control, or influence their infant soon after becoming a mother. Those early experiences influenced these women's views about child development. For example, all these mothers concluded that mothers are not solely responsible for their children's behaviors or personalities. For instance, before Alice had her first child, she believed that by reading many books she could learn how to raise her baby into "the Messiah." However, her early experience impacted this belief to the extent that she became resistant to the myth that mothers are solely responsible for how their children turn out:

> Here I had this baby that I was molding into the new Messiah, and I was thinking, "Wow!" (laughs) And then of course the Messiah grows up to be a holy terror! (laughs). And yet I have done everything right up to that point, like spanking was a no-no, and yelling was a no-no, and everything was a no-no. And we must absolutely raise him perfectly, and he was just like this holy terror! And I was thinking, "You know, maybe he's just the way he is."

> Maybe it's not, you know, it was nurture versus nature. Maybe nature has a little bit more of a say in some really weird ways.... So it changed my mind about nurture versus nature.... He's him, he's like, he's who he is.

In addition, for these women being the ever-present mother who is indispensable turned out not to be an option. Being around their babies all the time was too difficult, too demanding. They resisted this aspect of the discourse because they learned early in their experience that being ever-present was difficult for them. In these cases, resistance was triggered by the reality of being a mother. They realized that babies could be difficult to be around all the time, and that deciphering what they need and delivering it is nearly impossible. These types of experiences can motivate a new mom to begin to question the rosy picture painted by the discourse.

Because of how challenging children can be, being a full-time mother was difficult for many of the women. Ten women were explicit about their dislike of being the exclusive caregivers to their children. They did not like being mothers all the time. For example they said things like, "I would go crazy, I would put my head through the wall," "it was hell," or "it would mean loss of identity." These mothers expressed that being a full-time mother exclusively and not engaging in other work or other interests was very difficult. Prior to becoming mothers, they thought that having a baby would be solely a joyful experience and that they would want to be with their babies all the time. However, after having the baby, they realized that it could be a very difficult and painful experience at times, and decided that they would not follow the expectations of being full-time mothers.

Some women chose to be home with their children but did not necessarily agree with being focused only on their children. Other women believed that if they lived in more supportive communities, they would not have to be isolated or dedicate themselves exclusively to the care of their children. In sum, the actual experience of mothering influenced these women's views and practices around mothering. These experiences led them to resist the dominant beliefs that mothers should be ever-present, feel loving toward their children all the time, and feel solely fulfilled by being mothers.

A Mother's Personal Situation and History
Impact Her Ability to Resist

Women who resist may recognize that there are many factors that help them in their ability to resist and affect how much they are able to resist. Social supports such as partners, extended family, and friends, along with education, access to information, financial resources and social services, supportive employers and flexible work, easygoing children, and the Internet were identified by these women as helpful in being able to resist social expectations.

Partners

Many women in the study acknowledged that having partners who were involved made it easier for them to resist the dominant discourse of motherhood. They identified a variety of ways in which having a partner was helpful: having financial support freed some of these women to practice Attachment Parenting, research information in order to make informed decisions, home-school, avoid sending their children to daycare, or resist the "cult of materialism." These women were committed to sharing responsibility and viewed themselves as co-parents rather than mothers in the traditional sense of the word. Carla's words illustrate this point well: "I mean it's not like being a mother, it's like being a parent." Viewing themselves as co-parents freed these women not only to relieve themselves of some of the responsibility for their children, but also to resist the dominant discourse of motherhood by questioning and researching information that allowed them to make alternative choices.

These women also valued the emotional and moral support they received from their partners. Many of these women reported that their partners were supportive of their resistance and of their careers or interests. Having their partners' respect the way they mothered was described by many of the women as supportive of their resistance because it gave them a sense that they were doing the "right thing." Louise's words illustrate this example well. She considered that her husband's trust in her ability to parent their daughters in his absence allowed her to feel free to continue to mother in the way that worked for her:

> You see, he's not here all the time, so parenting and the leading role comes from me. Ah ... he doesn't fight that. He's not, 'Oh you don't know what you're talking about, blah, blah, blah'. He gives me a lot of respect about that.

In sum, partners who were supportive were viewed as helpful to these mothers' resistance. By sharing the responsibility for the care of their children or by being emotionally supportive, these partners helped these women to have more freedom to play other roles outside of mothering and to engage in other pursuits.

Access to friends

For most of the women I interviewed, having like-minded or supportive friends facilitated their resistance by providing encouragement and "an ear" regarding their experiences or views. Having friends that were accepting and non-judgmental and who would provide emotional support helped the women to deal with some of the challenges of resisting. Some of these mothers called a friend to say that they were angry and could not bear the frustration they felt toward their child. For example, Kate said, "Thank God, this one friend of mine, Mary, who took care of Ian before Brad was born, she was the most sane and positive. So every time I lost it, she would not see me as less of a being." Furthermore, friends who were willing to babysit allowed these women the time on their own that they so needed. Bonds with friends were also viewed as important relationships for the children who could benefit from the influence and love of other adults in their lives. For example, Theo explained that having other friends in her daughter's life was very important: "And so to make myself go do something so she can have a relationship with others is really, really important." On the flip side, those women who lacked like-minded friends, or whose friends were not always available, often felt isolated and judged.

A supportive extended family

The changing face of families in North American society has had an impact on mothers. Fewer families have access to extended family because in many cases they live too far to be able to participate in caring for, and spending time with, the children. Four of these women had families who helped consistently or occasionally with caregiving for their children. Grandparents, aunts, and uncles were available to babysit, pick up children at school, drive children to activities, and provide emotional and sometimes financial support; this made a big difference for these mothers. For example, Anna's in-laws helped by picking up her children from school at least once a week: "They know that on Thursday Grandma and Grandpa pick them up from school." These mothers explained that having supportive family members freed them to spend time away from their children, pursue their careers, or go out for an evening with their partners. They also valued the bonds that their children had developed with these family members. They felt that the more people who loved their children, the better.

Even though many of the women I interviewed did not have extended family nearby, they believed that having family close to them would be helpful in terms of freeing them to meet their needs. So that lacking supportive extended families in their communities forced them to be the only caregivers, in many cases along with their partners. For example, Astrid really wanted to pursue her interests and be involved in the community as an activist. She explained that if her mother and her sister lived in the same town, they would participate in her children's lives and this would free her to pursue some of those interests. Astrid had chosen to stay home with her children and mothered in what appeared to be an intensive mothering model because she lacked social supports to share the care of her children. She would have been happy to share her motherwork with others if they had been available. The interviews with these women suggest that resistance can be facilitated or hindered by access to others. We could ask then, are many mothers practicing intensive mothering out of choice or because, in our individualistic society, the task is left to her and her alone?

Education and access to information

Being educated was a factor that all but one of the women mentioned as one of the things that enabled them to challenge the expectations placed on them. Their education levels ranged from first year community college to doctoral studies. The women believed their education allowed them to know where to find research information in order to make informed decisions or to understand their experience better. Being educated also meant that they were able to evaluate the information they researched and discard what was not useful or realistic to them. Education also opened the door to specific types of employment that allowed some of the mothers to pay for quality daycare or babysitters, or work at home either part- or full-time. Education, then, was viewed as supportive of these mothers' resistance. They felt that being educated was an important aspect of their ability to question and critique information through ideological work and of their being able to find and research information.

Access to financial resources

None of the women I interviewed mentioned money as an issue in their lives at the time of the interview. Based on these women's examples, resistance to the dominant discourse of motherhood and the ideological work that accompanies it was not conditional on having a high income. The income levels for the 15 women I interviewed ranged from CAD $15,000 to over CAD $75,000. Three of the women were at the lowest end of the range and five at the highest. Those mothers with low income (Lilith, Aibrean, and Lisa) engaged in a process of resistance and did not appear to identify lack of financial wealth as affecting their ability to resist.

In addition, for some women, part of their resistance was against the "cult of materialism." In other words, they did not believe in pursuing lucrative careers in order to have more material goods. All the women met their basic needs for food and shelter. Lilith, a single 23-year-old mother of toddlers, however, was concerned about losing her daycare subsidy due to ongoing government cutbacks. Her annual income was between CAD $15,000 and CAD $30,000. She worried that she would have to withdraw from college if the government did not provide her with the subsidy and if the college peer support program—where she was employed—was also eliminated. She emphasized that she was able to resist being a full-time mother by pursuing her interests because of this financial assistance. Having access to financial resources—whether provided by a partner, personal employment, or government subsidies—allowed these women to make choices that worked for them; it enabled them to meet their needs, pursue careers, or stay home with their children.

Access to supportive/flexible employers or work

For many of the women who worked outside of the home, having less stress because they had an employer that was supportive and flexible was helpful to their resistance. Being able to work flexible hours at a job they enjoyed, and that took them out of the house, and provided stimulation was very important for many of these women. Flexibility in the terms of their employment allowed these women to have more time to meet their own needs, which was central to their resistance. In sum, being able to work at home everyday or some days of the week, or to work part-time at a job that relates to one's career, was important to feeling like "having the best of both worlds" particularly when it was combined with partners who co-parented.

"Easygoing" children

Some of the women mentioned that the personalities and temperaments of their children were an important factor that made it easier for them to resist. These women believed that having children who cooperated and were easygoing facilitated their ability to resist because they did not have to attend to them all the time. This is an important point because as some of these mothers explained, some of their children's personalities or temperaments were intense, emotional, and difficult to soothe. Health issues or disabilities may have affected others. Easygoing personalities, liking daycare, keeping themselves entertained, and being independent were all descriptors used by these women to illustrate how the temperament of their child "made it easier" for them to continue to resist. Having children who were easy going and easy to parent helped these mothers' resistance because these children did not demand too much attention and care. Kate, for example, said, "I give a lot of credit to my kids for making it work too." Children who need more attention, care, and supervision may make it more challenging for a mother to resist particularly if she lacks social supports. Aibearn's son who had ADHD, needed a significant amount of attention during the after school hours. So Aibearn explained that she took time for herself in the mornings when he was away at school and when her baby slept or was otherwise entertained.

Access to social services or outside resources

Many of the women found that support groups for mothers and their children were validating of their experiences and helped them to stay on their path of resistance. La Leche League, for example, was a source of support for some of the mothers who chose to breastfeed. These women found this type of support helpful particularly when they breastfed their children for an extended period of time. They believed that practicing extended breastfeeding resisted the mainstream expectation that a mother will not breastfeed longer than a year. They found that La Leche

League was supportive of their resistance by normalizing this choice for them. Nancy met some very supportive friends at La Leche League when she lived in Washington, D.C.: "I ended meeting these women, the most amazing group of women, that I have to this day met." Parent and tot playgroups also provided a source of support for some of the women. These women found that the groups were forums to discuss and vent their frustrations in non-judgmental environments. For some of these women, these early group experiences shaped their views of motherhood, and encouraged them to continue to resist and question societal norms and expectations.

There were two mothers who disliked parent and baby groups. These women felt that the women in these groups only talked about topics that related to babies and this was frustrating to them because they wanted to engage in other types of conversations. For example, Theo chose not to go to baby groups because she wanted to talk about other issues that did not relate to mothering or children and found that other women were unwilling to do so. These examples illustrate the diversity of what these women found helpful, how they resisted, and how they experienced various aspects of mothering.

Access to good daycare service or caregivers

Some of the women preferred not to take their children to daycare, which does not appear to be resistant of the discourse but compliant. Five of the women, however, were comfortable with taking their children to daycare. It was nevertheless important to them that daycare providers were qualified and caring. If Kate's' children liked the babysitter, she was happy to hire them: "They may not be the most experienced, but if they really click with my kids they will baby sit." She described herself as easygoing and not needing to be "picky" about it.

For these women, having access to good paid caregivers meant that they could then pursue their interests and careers without worrying about their children. These women resisted the dominant discourse of motherhood because they did not see themselves as having to be present all the time. Having good alternative caregivers freed the women to balance being with their children and pursuing personal interests or needs. These women also believed that exposing their children to other adults was a positive experience for their children because the children could then learn from many different adult styles and caregiving patterns. With extended families often not nearby and women unable to afford or choosing not to be stay-at-home mothers, having access to paid, competent caregivers is very important. In countries like the U.S. and Canada, governments have refused to provide universal daycare for children, the consequence of which burdens lower income mothers and their families.

Use of the Internet as support

The Internet has revolutionized the ways that mothers connect with one another, find like-minded women, and speak about their experiences. Many of the mothers in the study shared that the Internet provided them with a sense of connection to other like-minded women. The women I interviewed mentioned various websites such as hipmamma.com, youarestillhere.com, and ezboard.com. They visited the websites as an opportunity to meet other women and to voice their concerns, frustrations, and joys as mothers. Their use of the Internet facilitated these women's resistance because, in finding other women who thought like them, they were able to find support for their views about mothering. They found that they did not have to censor what they said to others because other users were supportive, non-judgmental, and like-minded.

Furthermore, these websites allowed many of the users to learn about social issues that relate to mothers and their children. Alice also belonged to a writers' website where she shared her work and talked with other writers. Aibrean mentioned that when she was a single mother and university student, it was the Internet that "saved [her] life" because she felt lonely and isolated. Some of the women also used the Internet as a source of information. All of the women had email addresses and used this service regularly. This medium may hold some possibilities in helping women communicate honestly about the realities of being a mother and in finding support in resisting. A search on Facebook reveals several sites of women who are supporting each other in navigating motherhood: Moms who Like Wine, Hip Mothers, Hip Mommas, and Moms Like Me.

Of course, this same medium is full of examples that uphold the dominant discourse of motherhood. It is possible that these women's education assisted them in evaluating the validity of the information they encountered on the Internet or in other types of media.

Early Experiences May Influence Resistance

Mothers

All of the women mentioned some sort of early influences on the way they mothered. None of the women were prompted to speak about their mothers, but when asked what they thought had influenced them in terms of their own mothering and in particular their resistance, they mentioned their mothers. For some, their mothers were a source of inspiration and guidance. These women described their mothers as "fair," "inspirational," "just," as someone "who valued equality between men and women," or who "was not in your face."

Other women perceived their mothers as "sacrificial," someone who "gave and gave and gave," "not doing what she wanted to do but what others expected her to," "being too focused on me," "screwed up," or being overly focused on "cleaning and cooking." These women did not want to make the same choices as their mothers. They often engaged in exploring the options that were available to them as mothers with the purpose of not being as sacrificial as their mothers. This supported their process of resistance examining their mothers' sacrifices or choices contributed to these women resisting becoming the sacrificial mother themselves.

Some unique stories emerged that related to how early life experiences were influential on their mothering experience. Two of the women were adopted. They both sought and found their biological mothers after they had themselves become mothers. They were the only two women who said that caregivers should be blood relatives if possible because in this way they are more invested in the children's well-being.

Three of the women's mothers had passed away, an experience which also influenced these women's choices and experiences. These three women expressed that it was important for them to see that their children had connections to others other than them. They felt a significant loss when their mothers died and feared that this could happen to their children. This experience influenced their views on being the central person in their children's lives. They resisted the belief that mothers should be the main and sole caregivers because this limits the bonds that children can have with others should their mother die. They felt that it was important that others be close and influential in their children's lives because as Jane said, "Just in case it happens to me, I don't think about it all the time but I do think about it. I don't want the bottom to fall out of their lives, the way it did for me." To summarize, the women's mothers influenced their mothering practices to varying degrees and some often resisted the idea that mothering should be sacrificial in part because of how they viewed their own mothers' practice of mothering.

Fathers/Parents

Only two women mentioned their own fathers and four women mentioned their parents as influencing their resistance. One participant perceived her father as a good role model, while another participant's father was a negative force. Parents were mentioned as being a good influence, "with a wonderful foundation of values," being good cooks and housekeepers, never fighting, or "very screwed up people." Women stated that in some cases they wanted to emulate their parents/father but in many other cases they wanted to ensure that they did not make the same mistakes as their parents/father. Catherine who viewed her father as a negative influence, made an effort to choose a different kind of partner, one who would be supportive, involved, and a good influence on her children. For these women, thinking about their families and how they impacted them influenced their mothering practices and their resistance. It appears that this process contributed to their conviction that what they are doing as mothers is good for their children and for them.

Awareness of Social Structures Was Influential in the Desire/Choice to Resist

Many of the women talked about various social structures, norms, and ideologies that impacted women and mothers. Some indicated that their choices were either supported, limited, or blocked by the way society is structured. Anna's words illustrate this point well:

> *I guess the one thing that I guess is influential as well, is the period of time in which I'm being a parent. Just the fact that it was socially acceptable for women to work, made it, you know...on the whole, I mean other women work ... so it didn't feel like it was abnormal or the wrong thing to do. And I believe that 50 years ago it would have been a different story.*

Some women voiced their frustration with society's belief that what mothers do is not considered "work," how patriarchy places mothers in a position to have to choose between being with their children and working, and with the lack of a community of care-givers. Madelaine expressed that it is difficult for her to make sense of her mothering work as work. She felt that her experience is affected by society's lack of mechanisms to allow women the freedom to make the choices that work for them:

> *I don't know, women take on this role, and they don't like it but they're expected to do it.... Feminism has allowed us to think that, you know, given us the power to realize that this is not how it has to be. But it has yet to have the mechanisms in place to allow it to be different.*

Many of the women also emphasized the lack of community and social support for mothers and children. These mothers made it very clear that staying home with children is not what oppresses women. To them it was society that isolates mothers and does not consider their work as a valuable contribution. This was at the core of how motherhood is devalued and because it is devalued, society continues to add to the burden without offering any sup-port, recognition, or consideration for mothers' needs.

Furthermore, these women found it frustrating that society did not provide them with quality care or communities where a vari-ety of caregivers could be available. Kate's story is a rare example of how community support can free mothers from having to be ever-present. When Kate lived in co-operative housing in East Vancouver, she experienced a sense of support and freedom for her children because the safety of the children while they played was a responsibility that was shared by the whole community. All the parents kept an eye on the children who played in an enclosed courtyard; Kate found this to be how society should be structured. There were many benefits to this type of co-op community. As Kate explained, children were able to play freely and safely, but also parents and the whole community often shared time together, which developed close relationships among them. This type of community was the perfect setup for parents to have spontaneous potluck dinners and to exchange babysitting favours with one another. To Kate, this was the ideal living situation for mothers because they received ongoing support from others in the community. She explained, however, that she was aware that this type of community is not available for most parents. Kate stated that the lack of community for most mothers is what makes it stressful to be a mother.

Being aware of social structures and social discourses led these women to look outside of their private lives to understand their experience and to place some of the responsibility for the limitations in their lives on the larger society within which they lived. Their resistance in this case was related to being active in questioning the status quo and not feeling that they were to blame for everything relating to their children or for their failure to always meet the demands placed on them. They believed that women are overwhelmed largely because of how society is structured and how it promotes many practices and beliefs that are inconsiderate of mothers.

What has been demonstrated is that there are a variety of elements that interacted to form a place where these mothers were able to resist (Hacking, 1998). These elements relate to the women's experiences of mothering, to their current personal situations and early experiences, and in some cases to their awareness of social structures and discourses. Their resistance was not only influenced by these factors but also by the types of discourses from which they drew. These discourses influenced their choices and the social identities to which they adhered. Furthermore, these women's resistance was not a complete departure from the dominant discourse of motherhood. In every case, these women also conformed to aspects of the dominant discourse of motherhood.

Concluding Toughts on the Process of Resistance

The process of resistance to a dominant discourse is complex and multifaceted. The way these women navigated resistance and their perceptions of themselves and societal ideologies varied greatly. Some of the ideological work for these women was aimed at reconciling the interplay of various factors into a cohesive whole that made sense to them. The exploration of the various discourses from which the women in the study drew illustrates how resistance was complex and varied for each individual. None of the women resisted all of the dominant discourse of motherhood and none of them adhered fully to it.

It was interesting to see how they each challenged different aspects of the dominant discourse of motherhood to different degrees. Going into the study, I did not know how resistance would manifest itself. I was quite amazed at how none of them resisted *all* of the dominant discourse of motherhood in their approaches to mothering. Their experience was influenced by both the dominant discourse of motherhood and other alternative discourses. Of note, although resistance freed some of the women, it appeared to lead to more intensive mothering for others. For some of the women, their choice to resist the dominant discourse of motherhood involved Attachment Parenting, extended breastfeeding, and sleeping in the same bed with their children. Making choices based on the philosophy of Attachment Parenting resists some elements of the dominant discourse that promote independence in children from an early age. These women were resisting individualistic aspects of the discourse that promote independence in children while engaging in what appears to be more intensive mothering. On the other hand, some women subscribed to some aspects of the discourse of individualism, which led them to endeavour to raise children who were independent. This, in turn, freed them to have more independence and time away from their children. They resisted the belief that mothers need to be present at all times, while conforming to the dominant discourse of motherhood by holding the belief that children can be independent and develop relationships with others who care about them.

Another illustration of how resistance is complex relates to the belief that daycare is not the best choice for the caregiving of children. Some of the women resisted by meeting their own needs and having certain freedom from their children, but conformed to the discourse because they were only willing to leave their children in the care of other loving adults, and, in two cases, blood relatives were the most desirable. Others, however, resisted because they believed that meeting their needs and having freedom was important; they felt comfortable leaving their children in the care of daycare providers or babysitters. These two groups of women drew on different discourses that affected their practices regarding their children and themselves. In conclusion, resistance appeared to occur in degrees and in different forms. The ideological work or resistance in which the women engaged led them to different conclusions and practices. In the following and final chapter, I engage in a thoughtful discussion of what the study may mean for mothers, social change, and for those who hope to advance our own understanding of mothering and resistance.

Chapter 7

Through the Maze of Motherhood: Weaving Experiences of Resistance

So for me it's imperative to be the kind of mother that I want to be—to not be a mother all the time. I guess that sums up a lot of my beliefs about mothering. —Jane

In the 1986 edition of *Of Woman Born*, Adrienne Rich emphasizes that a collective movement needs to go beyond simply pointing out that the institution of motherhood is oppressive to women and highlights how crucial women's empowerment is for mothers. Rich suggests that motherhood has two meanings: "the potential relationship of any woman to her powers of reproduction and to children; and the institution, which aims at ensuring that the potential shall remain under male control" (1986, p. 13). Rich argues that mothering itself is not the problem for women but that the social construction of motherhood, which is aimed at controlling and oppressing them, is what burdens them. Of particular note, Rich emphasized that mothers can transform patriarchal motherhood into empowered mothering by reclaiming their power through their practices as mothers. The resistant mothers I speak about in this book did just that. They practiced empowered mothering and reclaimed some of their power by resisting and developing their own maternal practices. In this chapter, I provide some final thoughts about their experience of resistance, their agency and sense of empowerment, the interplay of the discourses they drew from, and the importance of honouring all mothers' needs and worthiness.

The women who shared their stories with me regained some of this power by engaging in a process of resistance against the dominant discourse of motherhood. I wrote this book hoping that their stories would help mothers find ways to free themselves from the oppression and restricted potential that results from the dominant discourse of motherhood. My message is not prescriptive but rather an expansion of the possibilities for mothers, providing a window into the complexities of resistance and the lived experience of women who view themselves as resisting. It is important that mothers come to understand the process and benefits of resistance. A review of the literature uncovered little previous knowledge about the *experience* of resistance, not only for mothers but for other groups as well. Resistance involves critiquing dominant and alternative discourses, choosing among the various alternative discourses, and integrating these with past and present experiences to develop a particular set of beliefs, practices, and actions.

In this book, I provide a portrait and interpretation of the multifaceted ways in which certain women who were engaged in the activity of mothering practiced various forms of resistance. If I was to suggest that this study has uncovered the ideal way to mother, I would be perpetuating the very premise I am challenging: that there is one right way to mother. The purpose of the original study was not to offer another grand narrative on the best way to mother. Rather, the findings suggest that there are many possible ways to mother and that resisting dominant discourses is a complex process where women find themselves navigating among multiple and competing ideologies.

Another important aim of this book is to challenge feminist theories of mothering that portray mothers as victims of discourses, unable to be active agents in their own lives (Garey, 1995; Hays, 1996; Rich, 1986). The mothers in my study resisted and in doing so, they constructed alternative experiences and practiced personal agency. Until recently, much of the literature on mothering documented that mothers live under a dominant discourse that promotes feelings of inadequacy (Thurer, 1994), depression (Mauthner, 1999; Stoppard, 2000), and confusion (Hays, 1996) in many mothers. This literature often portrayed mothers as powerless victims of the dominant discourse that encourages them to live up to an ideal that is difficult, if not impossible, to achieve. In contrast, the experiences of the women I interviewed suggest that by drawing on alternative discourses and seeing themselves in certain ways, they were able to be agents of choice in their own lives.

My journey through the analysis of the interviews was like weaving a cloth with many threads and patterns. The process of resistance is like that; each mother wove her own reality by drawing on alternative and dominant discourses, by relying on her resources, aligning herself with various social identities, and using her own personal experiences of mothering and being parented herself. The weaving is empowering but challenging at times. I end this book by again weaving the women's stories, their experiences of resistance, and the overall findings with some final thoughts and hopes. In discussing and highlighting various aspects of resistance and positioning the findings in the context of other feminist research and theory, I hope to encourage further thought and conversation. I first turn my attention to the aspect of resistance, agency, and empowerment.

The concept of agency is central because mothers are not necessarily passive victims of discourses, but may be active agents in their own lives. It is through this agency that women are able to resist and experience a sense of empowerment. In other words, resistance is possible because human beings can exercise agency, which is the capacity to act and to respond to life's problems. Although agency is necessary to the process of resistance, it is important to note that agency does not always include acts of resistance. Our agency is exercised in the choices we make in how we run our lives.

In a process of ideological work and critical analysis, the women in the study questioned and critiqued social ideas and structures in order to make more satisfying personal and mothering choices. The women I interviewed exercised their power by shaping their own lives and generating some of their own practices and social relations. Similar to the feminist mothers in Gordon's (1990) and Green's (2009) studies, these women did not see themselves as "downtrodden, depressed victims of circumstances; [or as] passive recipients of society's dictums" (Gordon, p. 64). Moreover, resistance, as an outcome of agency, activates mothers and creates a sense of empowerment.

Resistance is a complex process that does not exist outside of societal discourses and involves the interplay of various factors such as critical thinking and decision-making. Resistance is delimited by the various discourses available at any point in history. Mothers draw from a multitude of discourses to explore what is most meaningful to them but they do not instantly "invent" new and original discourses. However, new discourses may emerge over time as more and more women resist and create new ways to conduct themselves as mothers. Mothers also draw on discourses that allow them to construct alternative views and practices, but how much they can deviate from the dominant discourse of mothering is limited by serving competing and contradictory discourses.

The concept of "constrained" agency is helpful to contextualize this. Agency is always limited by the discourses that exist at any one time (Charrad, 2010; Day, Johnson, Milnes, and Rickett, 2010). This does not mean that we cannot have agency, but that agency is restricted by the discourses that shape us (Emirbayer and Mische, 1998; Foucault, 1978). Therefore, resistance is constrained by the current discourses available and it is within these discourses that mothers must find ways to resist.

Resistance is not black or white; we can't divide mothers into those who resist and those who don't, or define those who resist as completely outside the dominant discourse. The women who I interviewed resisted many aspects of the dominant discourse but also complied with other aspects of the same discourse. This is an important aspect of the process of resistance. It raises the possibility that we cannot resist a discourse in its totality; we may resist aspects of it, but because we live in a society that has socialized us within its discourses and values, we absorb parts of it. We continue to buy into aspects of the dominant discourse even when we have caught on to its myths and unfairness.

In my case, I still become worried when my adult daughters need me. I am not always sure how much I should still "help" them with their life problems. I have a difficult time drawing a boundary between my needs and theirs. Both my values as an empowered mother and those from the dominant discourse of motherhood to which I still reluctantly hold on to—that I must love them unconditionally, that sometimes I need to sacrifice for them, that they *need* me—continue to be at play in how I interact with them.

When I began the study, I was naïve in that I thought I would find radical rebel mothers who completely rejected the dominant discourse of motherhood. When I met with them and analyzed the interviews, it became apparent that, even for those who considered themselves feminist, the dominant beliefs about motherhood and children were still present within their beliefs and practices. One excellent example of this struggle to resist while also being influenced by the dominant discourse of intensive mothering, is contained in Lynn O'Brien Hallstein's article, "Second Wave Silences and Third Wave Intensive Mothering" (2008). In writing about her own experience as a feminist mother, she begins her article with these words: "Every day feminist mothers must negotiate the complex struggle between intensive and empowered mothering" (p. 107). In a candid voice, O'Brien Hallstein speaks about being a feminist mother who found herself surprised by the fact that along with her feminist mothering, she was also practicing aspects of intensive mothering. She offers some revealing examples of sacrificing her job to care for her children, loss of personhood through giving into her role of sacrificial mother, and silencing herself around more traditional mothers. Some of her sacrifice involved putting her son's needs ahead of her own because this, she thought, was essential to "good mothering."

O'Brien Hallstein, like the women in my study, resisted and yet also conformed to the dominant discourse of motherhood. In her journey, she concludes that it is important that mothers honour their personhood (i.e., being a person with her own life, desires, dreams, aspirations, and needs, rather than just a mother) and their right to mother their own empowered way. And yet, her story and those of the women I interviewed suggest that our agency and resistance are constrained by dominant and alternative discourses (Foucault, 1978). In understanding the process of resistance, we must recognize that mothering practices occur in a myriad of combinations of the dominant discourse of motherhood and other alternative discourses.

One finding of note is the fact that *perceived* resistance appeared to be as important as actual resistance in contributing to these mothers' experience of empowerment. Even when their resistance did not translate into alternative mothering practices, due often to the structural and pragmatic realities of their lives, it was empowering for these women to go against the mainstream thereby positioning themselves as agents rather than victims of society's dictates. All of the participants saw themselves as resisting. And yet, some of their resistance involved practices that appeared to lead to more intensive mothering.

Take for example Astrid, who had chosen to practice Attachment Parenting and the family bed. As mentioned before, Attachment Parenting promotes the idea that mothers must keep close contact with their children in order to develop secure, close attachments (Sears and Sears, 2001). Mothers must endeavour to spend copious amounts of quality time loving, caring, and being affectionate with their children. Astrid was adamant that Attachment Parenting did not make her a "doormat" or a passive, traditional mother; she was a resistant mother who considered her struggles related to mothering in isolation from others and because she lacked community around her. Although her mothering appeared to be conforming to the dominant discourse in this regard, she still felt she was resisting, and therefore, felt empowered. This speaks to the complexity of resistance and to how it is *perceived resistance* that leads to an experience of empowerment, and not necessarily what or how a mother resists.

The process of resisting dominant discourses is also laden with challenges. Although resistance is empowering and it enhances a woman's sense of self, it does not come without its trials. The women I spoke with had to endure criticism from others. Because the dominant discourse dictates the model of mothering against which all mothering practices are evaluated (Medina and Magnuson, 2009), resistance is often faced with criticism and judgment. Resistance entailed having the courage to continue to resist while being subject to the gaze and judgment of others. Sadly it is usually other mothers who are the ones perpetuating the discourse by judging each other and expecting other mothers to practice sacrificial, intensive mothering.

The women I interviewed felt that they had to strategize intensely to participate in resistance and that resistance was more difficult in a society that is individualistic and unsupportive of mothers and children. Researchers, feminist advocates, and activists need to examine possible factors that could minimize the negative impact of resistance on mothers. We need to find ways for women who resist to not feel isolated or silenced, for resistance to involve a reduced degree of juggling and balancing, and for women of all socio-economic statuses to participate in the process of ideological work needed for resistance. In addition, we must explore which social changes may need to occur in order for women to mother in ways that deviate from the oppression of the dominant discourse.

All mothering is rewarding and taxing at the same time, and resistant mothering is no exception. Motherhood is pitted against a mother's right to honour her personhood and wellbeing (Maushart, 1999; O'Brien Hallstein, 2008). As Maushart suggests, motherhood is "infinitely profound and meaningful, more joyous and transcendent, yet more vexed and ambivalent, more downright dangerous, than we have yet dared to voice" (p. 244). When mothers are aware and conscious about the oppressiveness of the discourse, they may acknowledge the mask of motherhood. By acknowledging the mask of motherhood, mothers may be able to free themselves of guilt and confusion by knowing that the ambivalence, pain, and anger are valid feelings within the experience of mothering. In addition, being conscious may mean recognizing that we must stand up for our personhood. Maushart explains, "The feminist agenda has succeeded up to a point, and that point is motherhood. Beyond motherhood, our sexual politics remain more fraught and tense than ever, with both women and men staggering under a new weight of contradictory and extravagant expectations" (p. 243). The current tension, which is clear in the narratives of the women in this book, is between motherhood and personhood. Maushart emphasizes that the mask of motherhood relates to a collective denial that the question between motherhood and personhood exists at all. This question, however, is central to the process of resistance in which mothers not only honour their children but also equally honour themselves. In turn, honouring of our personhood can enhance our sense of empowerment and agency.

An important finding of my study is that all of the women who participated felt a strong sense of empowerment. Some studies have documented that mothers often feel conflicted, alienated, frustrated, and inadequate, while at the same time they are afraid of harming their children (Boulton, 1983; McMahon, 1995). They also suggest that mothers frequently feel exhausted and depleted by the endless demands inherent in their mothering roles. In contrast, the mothers I interviewed felt proud of and empowered in their mothering roles. This enhanced sense of self appeared to be related to the fact that they perceived themselves to be resisting and questioning the dominant discourse of motherhood, making choices about how to mother based on their own beliefs and not on the dictates of society. In some cases, this meant they elected to engage in intensive mothering practices such as home schooling their children, while in others they elected to relinquish the primary care giving responsibilities to somebody else (i.e., their partner).

The critical issue for these women was making choices that were consistent with their own beliefs and values, and within the context of the structural realities and contexts of their own lives (e.g., lack of community, exclusive mothering). This is consistent with the experiences of the feminist mothers in Gordon's (1990) study, who benefited from being able to perceive, analyze, and criticize the social construction of motherhood, but who also experienced considerable structural challenges in their attempts to find alternative ways of practicing motherhood. Similarly, Fiona Green suggests that feminist mothers "are challenging motherhood and creating alternatives in mothering…"(2009, p. 4) and yet some of her participants also found mothering frustrating and disappointing because of the social pressures and barriers that patriarchal structures place on mothers. This suggests that the degree to which any mother can resist the "selfless mother" discourse and find alternate and more resistant ways to mother is limited by her context.

The women I interviewed derived a sense of empowerment simply from seeing themselves as resistant; what and how they resisted did not seem to make a difference: they all felt empowered. It seems that being aware of the social discourses and ideologies that oppressed them and questioning these in order to make conscious choices, contributed to their sense of empowerment. It is possible that from these feelings of empowerment, women can then begin to change the larger social structures by exposing the realities of being a mother and the importance of challenging social discourses that oppress and disempower them.

Empowerment opens up space for autonomy and authenticity

(O'Reilly, 2010). The women in my study endeavoured to be true to themselves, their families, and their parenting. They attempted to make decisions that were true to their own beliefs and values (Butterfield, 2010). In other words, these women's empowered mothering allowed them to experience a sense of autonomy in that they were making choices that contradicted the status quo while remaining true to their values. In her article, "Feminist Mothering," Andrea O'Reilly (2007) explains that authentic mothering may entail consciously resisting and rejecting patriarchal motherhood and telling the truth about the reality and the complexity of mothering. As both O'Reilly and Maushart (2000) suggest, authentic mothering is about refusing to live by the mask of motherhood and finding more authentic, autonomous ways of mothering. This authentic mothering, in turn, may allow mothers to practice mothering from a deeper place of empowerment and agency. The women in my study had caught on to the mask and refused to be controlled by societal expectations that disempowered them and impacted their autonomy.

Unlike the mothers who endeavor to adhere to the dominant discourse and aspire to live up to the ideal (Garey, 1995; Seagram and Daniluk, 2002), the mothers in my study positioned themselves in ways that supported them in struggling against mainstream definitions and expectations of good mothering. By seeing themselves as independent women and critical thinkers they claimed their individual right to choose their beliefs and practices around mothering. They appeared to be resisting the dominant discourse of motherhood by drawing on a discourse that promotes the rights of women who mother to have their own needs met, as opposed to subsuming or ignoring their needs in the exclusive service to their children. What is more, the more a mother believes in sacrifice and in the fragility of children, the more likely she is to experience feelings of guilt and inadequacy.

Given that much has been written and studied in regards to maternal guilt, it is important to highlight that the women in this study had a different experience that involved much less or no guilt at all. The literature on mothering suggests that trying to live up to the ideal may engender feelings of guilt for many mothers (Chodorow and Contratto, 1992; Eyer, 1996; Seagram and Daniluk,

2002; Thurer, 1994). Conversely, most of the mothers I interviewed reported rarely experiencing or being negatively impacted by feelings of maternal guilt. Rather than seeing themselves as sacrificial, selfless, all-giving mothers, the participants situated the problems they encountered *outside* of themselves and saw themselves in ways that opposed the dominant discourse.

Much of what has been written about the institution of motherhood places mothers in a constant state of self-doubt in which they often question whether their parenting choices are the most appropriate ones for their children. In contrast, most of the mothers I interviewed were generally very comfortable with their choices and the mothering decisions they had made. They felt *conviction* in their own knowledge and expertise as a result of their critiquing of the dominant discourse. Many mothers I have spoken to over the years have told me that they experience guilt. To them this is a "normal" part of being a mother. Guilt often controls them into more sacrifice and ultimately into depleting themselves. The fact that many of the women I interviewed did not experience that degree of guilt and in most cases none at all, suggests that resistance can be one way to safeguard against feelings of guilt. Feeling constantly that they are doing something wrong or not enough for their children is related to the dominant discourse, which sets mothers up to feel like they don't measure up or that they are never doing enough. Questioning the discourse may free women to exercise agency and conscious choice, which in turn may protect them from feelings of guilt and inadequacy.

This is another aspect of the empowering nature of resistance. It is possible that by seeing themselves as critical thinkers and by engaging in a process of questioning and arriving at their own conclusions, they protected themselves from the degree of self-doubt that other mothers reportedly experience. Mothering does not have to engender feelings of guilt and inadequacy, and these feelings can potentially be reduced or eliminated when mothers challenge societal messages that communicate that they are solely to blame for how their children turn out. By rejecting the idea that mothers are always the best caregivers of their children, that there is one acceptable way to mother, that mothers should always be present for their children, that they are to blame for anything that goes wrong with their children, and by sharing the responsibility of raising children with others, mothers may reduce their self-doubt and sense of responsibility thus reducing their feelings of guilt.

In addition to refusing to sacrifice their needs and values, these mothers' resistance was supported by certain personal and social resources—such as the support of partners, extended family members, friends, economic resources, and formal education—in negotiating and weakening the dominant discourse and opening up possibilities for resistance. Agency and indeed the ability to resist may be contingent not only on how a mother sees herself, but also on certain social and structural supports. Their stories reveal that resistance on the part of mothers may be supported or impeded by the structural and personal resources and realities of a woman's life.

Paternal involvement, for example, was one of the social supports that the women I spoke to reported as being very helpful to their resistance. Paternal involvement and extended family support is beneficial in reducing the burden and increasing the role and life satisfaction of women who are mothers (Baker, 2000; Kalmijn, 1999; Uttal, 1999). For example, in their exploration of the relationship between wives' reports of marital satisfaction and paternal involvement, Harris and Morgan (1991) found a high correlation between mothers' satisfaction and the degree of childcare involvement on the part of fathers. Similarly, the women I interviewed, whose husbands were extensively involved in caring for their children, expressed feeling satisfied with their lives because they believed they had "the best of both worlds." In other words, they were better able to balance their needs and those of their children.

Having partners who were actively involved in raising their children allowed these women to reconcile some aspects of the competing mothering and individualistic discourses. This is consistent with the findings of Baker (2000) who examined the experience of feminist mothers and their grown daughters. Baker found that the feminist mothers in her study, whose partners were significantly involved with childcare, did not experience conflict between motherhood and their feminist ideologies. The way the women I interviewed felt about their partners' contributions again draws attention to the importance of spousal involvement in the process of parenting children and the benefits of being able to share responsibilities of childcare and childrearing on women's efforts to resist the "selfless mother" discourse. It is important to highlight that all the women who were partnered in this study were in heterosexual relationships. The findings of my study do not uncover the dynamics of families with two mothers or other extended family members raising children. Future research should seek to understand how mothers in same-sex relationships divide childcare and motherwork and how these dynamics may differ or be similar to the process of resistance in heterosexual relationships.

In a similar vein, mothers generally benefit from the support of kin and friends. Many express a strong preference towards having their children cared for by relatives, particularly when their children are infants, toddlers, and in preschool (Uttal, 1999). The women I interviewed, although convinced that they were positioning themselves in opposition to the dominant discourse, complied with the larger societal discourse that promotes the idea that loving adults and family members are the ideal alternative to maternal care. Those participants who had access to kin for childcare appeared to experience the least conflict between motherhood and their alternative ideologies. This is important because it highlights that their resistance may be contingent on whether they perceive their children being loved by others.

One of the challenges that mothers in the Western world face today is juggling multiple roles to simultaneously meet the demands of full-time employment and full-time mothering (Gilbert, Holahan, and Manning 1981; Ranson, 1999). In other words, many mothers experience a tension between these competing demands. The women I describe in this book were no exception. They encountered tension among certain competing demands, specifically between how to meet their own needs, while also meeting the needs of their children. It was the experience of this tension that appeared to be at the centre of their juggling and balancing. These women juggled the various responsibilities inherent in their mothering roles, while still making space for their own needs and desires. In so doing, they felt they were making compromises and efforts guided by their own values and beliefs, and not because they were trying to be "perfect" mothers or "perfect" workers.

The values by which these mothers lived and conducted their lives appeared to be related to two competing discourses, the dominant discourse of motherhood and the discourse of individualism. Two social identities, those of the caring, responsible mother and the independent/individual woman were also at play. Having to navigate between these competing forces led these women to struggle in order to meet the demands of both. Thus, these women's stories suggest that mothers are forced to juggle among competing demands regardless of whether they resist the dominant mothering discourse (see Hays, 1996). The similarity between these women's stories and what is suggested in the literature implies that mothers, regardless of the degree of their resistance or adherence to the dominant discourse, must find a way to negotiate between two very powerful discourses. One discourse requires the sublimation of individual needs and rights in the service of children's needs, and the other promotes the rights of every individual to self-actualization. What seems unique to the women in this study was their ability to bridge this divide without feeling guilty about or doubtful of their maternal roles and performance.

On the topic of collectivity and community, I explore the following question: are many mothers practicing intensive mothering out of choice or because in our individualistic society the task is left to her and her alone? Some of the women who participated in my study explained that they were only mothering intensively because they were mothering in a society that did not support mothers and left mothers and families to be solely responsible for their own children. They saw society as individualistic and as not providing community and collectivity in the task of raising children. So the question remains, if we mothered in community, would the dominant discourse of motherhood have such power and reach? Is its power a direct result of our individualistic social structures? For example, Astrid was adamant that the lack of community was central to the issue of intensive mothering. She believed that mothers needed more collective efforts to help each other raise their children. Changing individualistic structures may be close to impossible, but mothers can join one another and create small collectives where they can share motherwork, and practice othermothering, as many African American women do.

The study sample included white women, all of whom had some post-secondary education; 13 were partnered; two were single; and one was single and gay but had only recently come out. Although this study may not reveal the process of resistance on the part of mothers who have not had access to post-secondary education, are sole support mothers, are from working and lower-income classes, or from different sexual orientations or ethnic backgrounds, it does begin to highlight the fact that resistance is possible and potentially beneficial for mothers. Andrea O'Reilly (2010), in "Outlaw(ing) Motherhood," writes, "Good mothers in patriarchal motherhood are defined as white, middle class, married, stay-at-home; while mothers from a politic of maternal empowerment are drawn from all maternal identities and include lesbian, non-custodial, poor, single, older, and 'working mothers'" (p. 21). This study is limited in that it does not provide a full portrait of mothers from these different backgrounds. However, it does plant the seed that suggests that resistance may be empowering to mothers. Future research might investigate what forms of resistance are possible for women from diverse backgrounds and social situations.

Consistent with feminist research (e.g., Wright, 2000), findings from my study suggest that formal education may help to promote and maintain resistance on the part of mothers. Most of the women in the study had some post-secondary education and mentioned access to information as enabling them to research possibilities and make alternative choices. In her article "Educated Mothers as a Tool for Change," Wright (2000) examined studies focused on women's education and social conditions in 18 nations. She concluded that women's education fosters women's equality and suggested that women's ability to access information, analyze new information, and argue their point of view promotes critical thinking that leads to questioning the status quo (i.e., dominant discourses). The findings of my study reflect Wright's conclusions in that the women believed that being educated helped them access and critique various sources of information regarding alternate mothering practices.

The question remains: how does social class or a lack of formal education manifest itself in the possibility of resistance? Do women who are working class, lower income, or have not attended post-secondary education resist differently? Do they resist less? Do they adhere to values that differ from those promoted by the dominant discourse of motherhood? Most of the literature on mothering suggests that there is a dominant discourse that is directed to all mothers. Yet, mothers from varying socio-economic backgrounds may feel differently about the discourse, their aspirations to meet the ideal may also vary, or the degree to which they buy into the discourse may be influenced by other factors. There is some evidence that suggests that most mothers are pressured and impacted by this dominant discourse. For example, Croghan and Miell (1998) found that mothers who were in the welfare or income assistance system felt they had been labeled as problem mothers and endeavoured to show that they were good mothers. These women drew on the discourse of the good mother to identify examples that suggest they were good mothers. At the same time they pointed to social and material circumstances that prevented them from parenting successfully, which would suggest that their parenting is based on the dominant discourse of motherhood.

This example suggests that mothers from various social classes, to some degree or another, are influenced by this dominant discourse. Croghan and Miell (1998) argued that the low income mothers they talked to were engaged in a process of resistance to the label of "problem mother." What was important to these women was to be seen more as the good mother, consistent with the discourse of motherhood. Some form of resistance may be found in all levels of society; however, the way women resist, what they resist, and how they experience resistance may vary considerably. Yet, Amy Middleton (2006) cautions against the idea that women who live in duress may be able to resist or practice empowered mothering given their situations. She discusses how feminist and empowered mothering may be difficult to practice by women who are living lives that are not deemed acceptable by society, who are lower class, who struggle with substance abuse or mental illness, or who find themselves in abusive relationships. She argues that these women would likely be more limited in acquiring states of authenticity, agency, autonomy, and authority than most educated mothers with access to needed resources. To support *all* mothers, more research needs to be conducted in order to tease out how we can best support their empowerment process.

All the women I interviewed resided in an urban area. If context affects experience, future research could explore the experience of mothers who resist in other social contexts such as rural or remote areas. Economies, communities, access to social resources, access to information, and other factors may differ from those of urban contexts, therefore leading to different forms of resistance. This type of inquiry would contribute to our knowledge of how different contexts and communities may impact a mother's resistance and whether different social structures are more or less conducive to this process.

The women's early mothering experiences, their observations of their own mothers, and their awareness of how society is structured also influenced their resistance. Feminists have explored and written extensively about the relationships between mothers and daughters and the influence of mothers on their daughters (Abbey and O'Reilly, 2000). The women I interviewed perceived their early life experiences to be significant influences on their mothering choices. They looked for ways in which they could mother more effectively by examining the impact that their own mothers and fathers had on them. This suggests that women who resist may seek answers to their mothering questions not only by questioning the status quo, but also by exploring their own early experiences and how these impacted them, both positively and negatively.

In addition, the current sociocultural context influences the mothering experiences of women who resist. The process of resistance is complex and is influenced by a variety of discourses and social identities. For the women I interviewed, resistance was influenced by the Western dominant discourses of individualism and self-actualization (Cushman, 1995; Kim, Triandis, Kagitcibasi, Choi, and Yoon, 1994). Individualism is present in societies where the ties between individuals are loose and people are expected to be responsible for themselves and their immediate family (Kim et al., 1994); it is based on cultures of separateness and self-actualization (Cushman, 1995). The larger dominant discourse of individualism in the past century has promoted an isolated, self-contained individual. During this period, there has been a decline in the proximity of extended families, so that the individual has become responsible for his/her own salvation through a search for self-actualization and growth (Cushman, 1995). These women drew significantly from these discourses to generate an empowered approach to mothering. Although many of them felt strongly that community and collectivity were important, they also drew from the discourse of individualism to justify their rights to choose and to be individuals. The participants felt it was unfair that they had to parent in isolation. In justifying this, they drew on a discourse of community as better for mothers. On the other hand, they drew on aspects of the individualism discourse to support other aspects of their resistance such as independence, the right to question, the right to make own choices (Kim et al., 1994). This highlights the complexity of resistance, where we can draw from and reject different aspects of the same discourse.

So the process of resistance entails resisting and conforming to various aspects of many discourses. To further illustrate the complexity of this web of discourses, I examine feminism and collectivity in the context of these women's resistance. First, the feminist discourse evolves from aspects of the larger individualistic dominant discourse that it critiques (Cushman, 1995). Feminism has blamed individualistic structures for the isolation of women into the private sphere, while encouraging women to become more collective (Rich, 1986). At the same time, it has drawn from individualistic discourses to promote the rights of women to make their own choices, such as the right to choose abortion. Thus, while calling for more collectivity amongst women, feminist discourse has employed the opposing larger individualistic dominant discourse to point to the rights of individual women. Similarly, in choosing a feminist individual rights discourse, the participants positioned themselves in opposition to the selfless mother discourse but were in essence drawing on yet another discourse that promoted a certain set of expectations.

Collectivist discourse places more emphasis on the goals and welfare of the group and promotes collective decision-making (Myers, 2000). Many of the women I interviewed identified collectivity as a possible answer to their isolation and intensive mothering practices. At the same time, they believed in their right to make their own decisions and were unwilling to involve paid caregivers in caring for their children. They perceived them as not being emotionally invested in their children, and therefore, not part of a trustworthy community. These mothers appeared to be largely influenced by the individualistic discourse so that their adherence to collective ideologies was limited to what they found reasonable within their individualistic beliefs and in so far as these were consistent with the "good mother" discourse (i.e., a good mother doesn't leave her children to be cared for by unrelated, paid caregivers). In sum, resistance involves reconciling tensions among discourses in order to weave our own fabrics of maternal practice.

Another lesson we can take from the stories of the women I interviewed is that mothers need to be valued and to have their needs considered just as important as those of their children. Adrienne Rich wrote in her book, *Of Woman Born* (1986) about times when she would pick up a book or the telephone to call someone while her child was occupied and entertained in his own world. But as soon as her son realized that she was in a world of her own that did not include him, he would immediately seek her attention. She felt this was "fraudulent, as an attempt to defraud [her] of living even for fifteen minutes as [herself]" (p. 23). She responded with anger and felt that her "needs always [had to be] balanced against those of a child, and always mine [are] losing" (p. 23). She emphasized, "I could love so much better, I told myself, after even a quarter-hour of selfishness, peace, of detachment from my children" (p. 23).

Adrienne Rich points to the reality of motherhood wherein mothers are not considered equal to their children. Why do children appear to be more valuable? Why are they celebrated as the human beings with most value? Part of mothers' resistance must consider whether mothers are of equal value to children. If that were so, how could mothers conduct themselves differently? They may, of course, have to meet their child's needs first when it is absolutely necessary (e.g., nighttime feeding, a sick child). However, the ideal of the perfect mother and the dominant discourse suggest that mothers must forget about themselves and sacrifice their every need in the name of their children's needs. How is it possible that in order to provide the optimum elements for one human being so many others must be sacrificed? How can this advance our overall well-being as a society? As we fight for equality between men and women, I would argue we must fight for equality between a child's value and that of its mother.

The mothers who participated in the study had made a commitment to balancing their needs with those of their children. This again speaks to the issue of personhood. As O'Brien Hallstein (2008) emphasized, mothers should honour and claim their right to maintain their personhood while honouring and caring for their children. The women who spoke to me felt that mothers do not have to do everything for their children to be loving. This suggests that love is not the same as sacrifice. We may need to redefine love and how it manifests itself. Bronwyn Davies and D'arne Welch at the University of New England suggest that mothers often feel that they are caught up in a contract of care that they cannot escape. We may consider Carol Gilligan's solution to this problem: reject the ethic of self-sacrifice and replace it with a morality of care that *includes mothers equally* with others (cited in Davies and Welch, 1986). If women have equal rights as any other human being, it follows that they have a right to have their needs considered and accommodated. What this means is that mothers should be willing and committed to do for themselves what they do for others. Some mothers have told me that this solution sounds good in theory but that they just don't have the time or resources to take care of their own needs in addition to those of their children. We may need to think creatively and historically to find ways of mothering that could equally meet mother and child needs.

If we believe in the ethic of care, we need to be part of that ethic; in other words, mothers deserve to matter as much as their children. Although being a mother does come with significant responsibility, it could be a more balanced experience. For example, mothers need more rest, fun, time for themselves, and team work at home. The point I want to make is that the dominant discourse of motherhood, which espouses the perfect mother, needs to be dismantled so that mothers can have better lives.

One important aspect of empowerment and affecting change may involve social action and activism. Some of the women in the study engaged in activism and worked to challenge the dominant discourse of motherhood. They did so even though the circumstances of their lives did not afford them the opportunity to share mothering responsibilities with significant others or to mother less intensively than they believed desirable for themselves and their children. The women I interviewed who elected to engage in social action felt that this was an important aspect of their resistance because it allowed them to step outside of the domestic boundary and to exercise their right to be heard. By moving themselves from the private sphere into the public realm, these women felt a sense of empowerment. I hope to encourage women and mothers to step into the public sphere, not only to become empowered, but also to develop a network of supportive others (Worrel and Remer, 1992).

Activists with access to social power because of their position as professionals, scholars, and writers must take special care not to promote the idea that there is one right way to mother. Many feminists and writers on the topic of motherhood have proposed feminist mothering as a possible model for mothers to become empowered and to transform patriarchal motherhood (Green, 2009; O'Reilly, 2004). However, empowered mothering may not involve feminist maternal practices, philosophies, or goals but could still impact change. Andrea O'Reilly (2004) suggested the following: "While we may not yet know completely what empowered [or feminist] mothering looks like, we, in interrupting and deconstructing the patriarchal narrative of motherhood, destabilize the hold this discourse has on the meaning and practice of mothering, and clear space for the articulation of counter narratives of mothering" (p. 12). This statement embraces many possibilities, whose foundation is to interrupt and deconstruct the dominant discourse. This was the starting point for the women I interviewed. They challenged, questioned, and in many ways interrupted the dominant discourse to open up space for counternarratives and practices.

Yet, their resistance in many instances was not based on a pure feminist mothering paradigm. Some saw themselves as feminist; some did not. Most drew on aspects of feminist discourse because it is part of our mainstream consciousness and not because they considered themselves feminists. They used the terms *empowerment* and *empowered* to describe their experiences of resistance. I would like to propose that we as scholars, feminists, and activists remain open and respectful of the various counter narratives and practices that may emerge as women become conscious about the discourse and engage in resistance. We do not want to propose that the best way to mother is feminist mothering, as we would be imposing yet another master discourse as the only way.

It may be useful to note that many of the factors that these mothers identified as supporting them in their resistance would likely be helpful to many mothers even if they did not seek to actively resist. I would venture to say that mothers would be less burdened if they had supportive families, partners, friends, and community; if they were educated or had access to financial resources; if they had supportive employers or were able to work from home; if they had access to good daycare or to solid social services that supported them and their children. Although these supports would make a difference in practical ways, those who still bought into the dominant discourse of motherhood would not experience the same sense of empowerment as those who consciously and actively resist it. We have a long way to go in creating a society that is supportive of mothers and that promotes ideologies that are pro-women and pro-mothers.

In spite of the potential limitations and pitfalls of the study, it nevertheless represents a valid portrayal of the experience and meaning of mothering for the women I interviewed, all of whom were actively resisting the dominant discourse of motherhood. Furthermore, the findings open a window to our understanding of possible personal and contextual factors that support the process of resistance for these women. I hope to contribute to the larger body of literature on the topic of mothering by suggesting that within the structural and contextual limits of their lives, mothers can be active agents in creating and living by more empowering and less restrictive mothering discourses and practices. Consistent with feminist theories, the findings of the original study reveal the possibility that mothers can challenge societal expectations and experience a sense of empowerment from doing so. More importantly, I hope to contribute to the lives of mothers by encouraging them to find avenues to mother in ways that are true to them, that empower them, and that improve their overall quality of life.

Bibliography

Abbey, S. and O'Reilly, A. (Eds.). (2000). *Mothers and daughters: Connection, empowerment, and transformation.* Lanham, MD: Rowman and Littlefield.

Adamson, N. et al. (1995). *Feminist organizing for change: The contemporary women's movement in Canada.* Toronto, ON: Oxford University Press.

Ainsworth, M., Blehar, M., Waters, E., Wall, S. (1978). *Patterns of attachment: A psychological study of the strange situation.* New York: Halsted Press.

Albanese, P. (2009). *Children in Canada today.* New York: Oxford University Press.

Albanese, P. (2010). Childhood. In A. O'Reilly (Ed.), *Encyclopedia of Motherhood* (pp. 205-210). Thousand Oaks, CA: Sage.

Alcoff, L. (1988). Cultural feminist, versus post-structuralism: The identity crisis in feminist theory. *Signs: Journal of Women in Culture and Society, 13* (Spring), 405-436.

Alexander, B. (2008). *The globalization of addiction: A study in poverty of spirit.* New York: Oxford University Press.

Aries, P. (1962). *Centuries of childhood: A social history of family life.* New York: Knopf.

Arnup, K. (1994). *Education for motherhood.* Toronto, ON: University of Toronto Press.

Azzara, J. (2001). Now more than ever: Unspoiling our kids. *Education Digest 67*(3) (November), 16-22.

Belenky, M. F., Clinchy, B. M., Goldberger, N. R., and Tarule, J. M. (1986). *Women ways of knowing: The development of self, voice, and mind.* New York: Basic Books.

Baber, K. M., and Allen, K. R. (1992). *Women and families: Feminist reconstructions.* New York: Guilford.

Badinter, E. (1981). *Mother love: Myth and reality.* New York: MacMillan.

Baker, C. (2000). Telling our stories: Feminist mothers and daughters. In A. O'Reilly and S. Abbey (Eds.). *Mothers and daughters: Connection, empowerment, and transformation.* New York: Rowman and Littelfield Publishers, Inc.

Beaujot, R. (2000). *Earning and caring.* Peterborough, ON: Broadview Press.

Bernard, J. (1974). *The future of motherhood.* New York: Dial Press.

Berry, M. (1994). *The politics of parenthood: Childcare, women's rights, and the myth of the good mother.* Toronto: Penguin Books.

Bespinar, F. U. (2010). Questioning agency and empowerment: Women's work-related strategies and social class in urban Turkey. *Women's Studies International Forum, 33,* 523-532.

Bobel, C. (2002). *The paradox of natural mothering.* Philadelphia, PA: Temple University Press.

Bowlby, J. (1991). *Attachment.* Toronto, ON: Penguin Books.

Bowlby, R. (2007). Babies and toddlers in non-parental daycare can avoid stress and anxiety if they develop a lasting secondary attachment bond with one caregiver who is consistently accessible to them. *Attachment and Human Development, 9*(4), 307-319.

Boulton, M. (1983). *On being a mother.* New York: Tavistock Publications.

Bradshaw. J. (1992). *Homecoming: Reclaiming and healing your inner child.* New York: Bantam Books.

Brown, L. M., Tappan, M. B., Gilligan, C., Miller, B.A., and Argyris, D. E. (1989). A reading for self and moral voice: A method for interpreting narratives of real-life moral conflict and choice. In M. J. Packer and R. B. Addison (Eds.), *Entering the circle: Hermeneutic investigation in psychology* (pp.141-164). Albany, NY: State University of New York Press.

Bronwyn, D. and Welch, D. (1986). Motherhood and feminism:

Are they compatible? The ambivalence of mothering. *ANZJS,* 22(3), 411-426.

Butterfield, E. (2010). Maternal authenticity. *Encyclopedia of Motherhood, 2,* 700-701.

Charrad, M.M. (2010). Women's agency across cultures: Conceptualizing strengths and boundaries. *Women's Studies International Forum, 33,* 517-522.

Chase, S. E., and Rogers, M. F. (2001). *Mothers and children: Feminist analyses and personal narratives.* New Brunswick, NJ: Rutgers University Press.

Chodorow, N., and Contratto, S. (1992). The fantasy of the perfect mother. In B. Thorne and M. Yalom. (Eds.), *Rethinking the family: Some feminist questions* (pp. 54-75). Boston: Northeastern University Press.

Christiansen, E. J., and Evans, W. P. (2005). Adolescent victimization: Testing models of resiliency by gender. *Journal of Early Adolescence, 25*(3), 298-316.

Cochran, L. (1985). *Position and nature of personhood: An approach to the understanding of persons.* Westport, CT: Greenwood Press.

Code, L. (1991). *What can she know? Feminist theory and the construction of knowledge.* London: Cornell University Press.

Comacchio, C. R. (1999). *The infinite bonds of family.* Toronto, ON: University of Toronto Press.

Contratto, S. (1984). Mother: Social sculptor and trustee of the faith. In M. Lewin (Ed.), *In the shadow of the past* (pp. 226-255). New York: Columbia University Press.

Coontz, S. (1992). *The way we never were.* New York: Basic Books.

Coontz, S. (1997). *The way we really are.* New York: Basic Books.

Cooper, D. (1994). Productive, relational and everywhere? Conceptualizing power and resistance within Foucauldian feminism. *Sociology, 28*(2), 435-445.

Corsaro, W. (1997). *The Sociology of childhood.* California: Pine Forest.

Croghan, R., and Miell, D. (1998). Strategies of resistance: Bad mothers dispute the evidence. *Feminism and Psychology, 8*(4), 445-465.

Cushman, P. (1995). *Constructing the self, constructing America:*

A cultural history of psychotherapy. Reading, MA: Addison-Wesley.

Davies, B. and Harré, R. (1990). Positioning: The discursive production of selves. *Journal for the Theory of Social Behavior,* *20*(1), 43-63.

Davies, B. and Welch, D. (1986). Motherhood and feminism: Are they compatible? The ambivalence of mothering. *Journal of Sociology, 22*(3), 411-426.

Day, K., Johnson, S., Milnes, K., and Rickett, B. (2010). Exploring women's agency and resistance in health related contexts: Contributors' introduction. *Feminism and Psychology, 20,* 238-241.

Devlin, V. (1995). *Motherhood: From 1920 to present day*. Edinburgh, Scotland: Polygon.

Dilaila, F. (1998). Daycare, child, and family influences on preschoolers social behaviors in a peer play setting. *Child Study Journal, 28*(3), 223-244.

Douglas, S. J. and Michaels, M. W. (2004). *The mommy myth: The idealization of motherhood and how it has undermined women*. New York: Free Press.

Duncan, S. (2005). Mothering, class and rationality. The Editorial Board of the *Sociological Review*. Oxford, England: Blackwell Publishing.

Edwards, A. E. (2000). Community mothering: The relationship between mothering and the community work of black women. *Journal of the Association for Research on Mothering, 2*(2), 87-100.

Eyer, D. (1996). *Motherguilt: How our culture blames mothers for what is wrong with society*. Toronto, ON: Random House.

Emirbayer, M. and Mische, A. (1998). What is agency? *American Journal of Sociology, 103* (4), 962-1023.

Fass, P. S. and Mason, M. A. (2000). *Childhood in America*. New York: New York University Press.

Forna, A. (1998). *Mother of all myths: How society molds and constrains mothers*. London: Harper Collins.

Fellman, A. C. (1985). *Perspectives on women: An introduction to women's studies*. Vancouver, BC: Simon Fraser University.

Foucault, M. (1978). *The history of sexuality: An introduction*. New York: Pantheon Books.

Foucault, M. (1984). *The Foucault reader*. New York: Pantheon.

Fox, B. (2006). Motherhood as a class act: The many ways in which "intensive mothering" is entangled with social class. In K. Bezanson and M. Luxton (Eds.), *Social reproduction: Feminist political economy challenges neoliberalism* (pp. 231-262). Montreal: McGill-Queens University Press.

Garey, A. (1995). Constructing motherhood on the night shift: Working mothers as "stay at home moms." *Qualitative Sociology, 18* (4), 415-437.

Gilbert, L. A., Holahan, C. K., and Manning, L. (1981). Coping with conflict between professional and maternal roles. *Family Relations, 30,* 419-426.

Glassner, B. (1999). *The culture of fear: Why Americans are afraid of the wrong things.* New York: Basic Books.

Gleason, M. (1999). *Normalizing the ideal.* Toronto, ON: University of Toronto Press.

Gomez, R. and McLearn, S. (2006). The association of avoidance, coping style, and perceived mother and father support with anxiety and depression among late adolescents: Applicability of resiliency models. *Personality and Individual Differences, 40*(6), 1165-1176.

Gordon, T. (1990). *Feminist mothers.* Basingstoke, Hampshire, England: Macmillan.

Green, F. (2009). *Feminist mothering in theory and practice, 1985-1995: A study in transformative practice.* New York: Edwin Mellen Press.

Green, R. (2005). Feminist mothering: Challenging gender inequality by resisting the institution of motherhood and raising children to be critical agents of social change. *Socialist Studies: The Journal of the Society of Socialist Studies, 1*(1), 83-101.

Greenberg, L., Rice, L. and Elliot, R. (1996). *Facilitating emotional change.* Toronto, ON: Guilford Press.

Greer, G. (1972). *The female eunuch.* New York: Bantam Books.

Gross, E. (1998). Motherhood in feminist theory. *Affilia, 13* (3), 269-272.

Hacking, I. (1998). *Mad travelers.* Charlottesville, VA: University Press of Virginia.

Hays, S. (1996). *The cultural contradictions of motherhood*. New Haven, CT: Yale University Press.

Harris, K. M. and Morgan, S. P. (1991). Fathers, sons and daughters: Differential paternal involvement in parenting. *Journal of Marriage and Family, 53*(3), 531-544.

Heatherington, E. M. and Park, R. D. (1986). *Child psychology*. New York: McGraw Hill.

Hillyard Little, M. (1998). Ontario mothers' allowance case files as a site of contestation. In F. Iacovetta and W. Mitchinson (Eds.), *On the case: Explorations in social history* (pp. 227-241). Toronto, ON: University of Toronto Press.

Hochschild, A. and Machung, A. (2003). *The second shift*. New York: Penguin Books.

Horwitz, E. (1998). *The experience of mothers in stepfather families*. Unpublished master's thesis, Simon Fraser University, Burnaby, BC.

Horwitz, E. (2003). Mother's resistance to the western dominant discourse on mothering. Unpublished doctoral thesis, University of British Columbia, Vancouver, BC.

Horwitz, E., and Long, B. (2005). Interrelationship of discourses on mothering and stress: A deconstruction. In M. Potter, (Ed.), *Mothering: Power and oppression* (pp. 97-110). Toronto, ON: Women's Press.

Huggins, R. and Huggins, J. (1996). *Auntie Rita*. Canberra, Australia: Aboriginal Studies Press.

Kadison, R. and DiGeronimo, T. F. (2004). *College of the Overwhelmed*. San Francisco: Jossey-Bass.

Kalmijn, M. (1999). Father involvement in childrearing and the perceived stability of marriage. *Journal of Marriage and the Family, 61*(2), 409-512.

Karen, R. (1990, February). Becoming attached. *The Atlantic Monthly*, 35-70.

Kim, U., Triandis, H. C., Kagitcibasi, G., Choi, S. and Yoon, G., (Eds). (1994). *Individualism and collectivism: Theory, method, and applications*. Thousand Oaks, CA: Sage.

Kinser, A. (2008). Thinking about and going about mothering in the third wave. In A. Kinser, (Ed.), *Mothering in the Third Wave* (pp. 1-16). Toronto, ON: Demeter Press.

Kinser, A. (2010). Feminism and mothering. In A. O'Reilly, (Ed). *Encyclopedia of Motherhood* (pp. 395-400). Thousand Oaks, CA: Sage.

Kofodimos, J. (1993). *Balancing act: How managers can integrate successful careers and fulfilling personal lives.* San Francisco: Jossey-Bass.

Kohut, H. (1971). *The Analysis of the self: A systematic approach to the psychoanalytical treatment of narcissistic personality disorders.* New York: International University Press.

Krause, N. and Geyer-Pestello, H. F. (1985). Depressive symptoms among women employed outside the home. *American Journal of Community Psychology, 13*(1), 49-67.

Kristal, J. (2005). *The temperamental perspective.* Baltimore, MD: Brooks Publishing.

Kruckman, L., and Smith, S. (1998). An introduction to postpartum illness. *College of Humanities and Social Sciences, Indiana University of Pennsylvania.* Retrieved on June 25, 2001, from the World Wide Web: http://www.chss.iup.edu/postpartum/preface.html.

Lincoln, Y. S., and Guba, E. G. (1986). But is it rigorous? Trustworthiness and authenticity in naturalistic evaluation. *Naturalistic evaluation: New directions for program evaluation, 30,* 73-84 .

Little, D. L. (1999). Independent workers, dependable mothers: Discourse, resistance, and AFDC workfare programs. *Social Politics, 6*(2), 161-202.

Mahoney, M. A. and Yngvesson, B. (1992). The construction of subjectivity and the paradox of resistance: Reintegrating feminist anthropology and psychology. *Signs, 18*(18), 44-73.

Marshall, K. (2006). Converging gender roles. *Canadian Economic Observe* 7 (7). (extracted from Statistics Canada website <http://www.statcan.gc.ca/pub/75-001-x/10706/9268-eng.htm>.

Martin, J. and Sugarman, J. (2001). Interpreting human kinds: Beginnings of a hermeneutic psychology. *Theory and Psychology, 11*(2), 193-207.

Maushart, S. (2000). *The mask of motherhood: How becoming a mother changes our lives and why we never talk about it.* New York: Penguin Books.

Mauthner, N. (1999). Feeling low and feeling really bad about feeling low: Women's experiences of motherhood and post-partum depression. *Canadian Psychology, 40*(2), 143-161.

Mauthner, N. (2010). I wan't being true to myself: Women's narratives of postpartum depression. In D. Jack, and A. Ali. (Eds.). *Silencing the self across cultures: Depression and gender in the social world* (pp.459-484). New York: Oxford University Press.

Mawami, F. N. (2001). *Sharing attachment practices across cultures: Learning from immigrants and refugees.* Toronto, ON: St. Joseph's Women's Health Centre.

McCartney, K., and Philips, D. (1988). Motherhood and childcare. In B. Birns and D. F. Hay (Eds.), *The different faces of motherhood, 157-182.* New York: Plenum Press.

McMahon, M. (1995). *Engendering motherhood.* New York: Guilford Press.

Medina, S. and Magnuson, S. (2009). Motherhood in the 21st century: Implications for counselors. *Journal of Counseling and Development, 87,* 90-97.

Middleton, A. (2006). Mothering under duress: Examining the inclusiveness of feminist mothering theory. *Journal of the Association for Research on Mothering, 8*(1,2), 72-82.

Mikulincer, M. and Florian, V. (1999). The association between parental reports of attachment style and family dynamics, and off-spring's reports of adult attachment. *Family Process, 38*(2), 243-257.

Morse, D. R. and Furst, M. L. (1982). *Women under stress.* New York: Van Nostrand Reinhold.

Myers, D. (2000). *The American paradox: Spiritual hunger in an age of plenty.* New Haven, CT: Yale University Press.

Nelson, M. (2010). *Parenting out of control: Anxious parents in uncertain times.* New York: New York University Press.

Neufeld. G. (2000). Creative Parenting (lectures). Vancouver, British Columbia.

Neufeld, G. and Mate, G. (2006). *Hold on to your kids: Why parents need to matter more than peers.* New York: Ballantine.

Nicolson, P. (1993). Motherhood and women's lives. In D. Richardson and V. Robinson (Eds.), *Introducing women's studies:*

Feminist theory and practice (pp. 201-223). New York: Mac-Millan.

Nicolson, P. (1998). *Post-natal depression: Psychology, science and the transition to motherhood*. New York: Routledge.

Nicolson, P. (1999). Loss, happiness, and post-partum depression: The ultimate paradox. *Canadian Psychology, 40*(2), 162-178.

O'Brien Hallstein, L. (2008). Second wave silences, third wave mothering. In A. Kinser (Ed.), *Mothering in the Third Wave* (pp. 107-118). Toronto, ON: Demeter Press.

O'Brien Hallstein, L. (2006). Conceiving intensive mothering. *Journal of the Association for Research on Mothering, 8*(1,2), 96-108.

O'Reilly, A. (2004). *Mother outlaws: Theories and practices of empowered mothering*. Toronto, ON: Women's Press.

O'Reilly, A. (2006a). *Rocking the cradle: Thoughts on motherhood, feminism and the possibility of empowered mothering*. Toronto, ON: Demeter Press.

O'Reilly, A. (2006b). Between the baby and the bathwater: Some thoughts on a mother-centred theory and practicing of feminist mothering. *Journal of the Association for Research on Mothering, 8*(1,2), 323-330.

O'Reilly, A. (2007). Feminist mothering. In A. O'Reilly (Ed.), *Maternal Theory: Essential Readings* (pp. 759-785). Toronto, ON: Demeter Press.

O'Reilly, A. (2010). Outlaw(ing) motherhood: A theory and politic of maternal empowerment for the twenty-first century. *Hecate, 36* (1,2), 17-29.

O'Reilly, A. (Ed.). (2011). *The 21st century motherhood movement: Mothers speak out on why we need to change the world and how to do it*. Toronto, ON: Demeter Press.

Piaget, J. (1952). *The origins of intelligence in children*. New York: International University Press.

Piaget, J. (1960). *The child's conception of the world*. London: Routledge.

Polasky, L. J. and Holahan, C. K. (1998). Maternal self-discrepancies, interrole conflict, and negative affect among married professional women with children. *Journal of Family Psychology, 12*(3), 388-401.

Pollock, K. (1988). On the nature of social stress: Production of a modern mythology. *Social Science Medicine, 26*(3), 381-392.

Porter, M. (2010). Focus on Mothering. *Hecate, 36*(1,2), 5-12.

Ramazanoglu, C. (1989). *Feminism and the contradictions of oppression*. New York: Routledge.

Ranson, G. (1999). Paid work, family work, and the discourse of the full time mother. *Journal of the Association for Research on Mothering, 1*(1), 57-66.

Reifman, A., Biernat, M. and Lang, E. (1991). Stress, social support, and health in married professional women with small children. *Psychology of Women Quarterly, 15*, 431-445.

Rich, A. (1986). *Of woman born*. New York: W.W. Norton.

Robinson, S. and Robinson, L. (1998). Challenging the connection of mother-daughter relationships: A deconstruction of the discourse. *Canadian Women's Studies/les cahiers de la femme, 18*(2,3), 64-65.

Rountree, C. (2000). *On women turning 30: Making choices, finding meaning*. San Francisco: Jossey-Bass.

Ruddick, S. (1983). Maternal thinking. In J. Treblicot (Ed.), *Mothering: Essays in feminist theory* (pp. 213-230). Totowa, NJ: Rowman and Allanhead.

Scott, J. (1990). Deconstructing equality-versus-difference: Or, the uses of poststructuralist theory for feminism. In A. Hirsh (Ed.), *Conflicts in feminism* (pp. 134-148). New York: Routledge.

Scott, J. (2001). Fantasy echo: History and the construction of identity. *Critical Inquiry, 27*(2), 284-315.

Seagram, S. and Daniluk, J. C. (2002). It goes with the territory: The meaning and experience of maternal guilt for mothers of preadolescent children. *Women and Therapy, 25*(1), 61-89.

Sears, A. (2001). *Of diapers and dissertations: The experiences of doctoral student mothers living at the intersection of motherhood and studenthood*. Unpublished doctoral dissertation, University of British Columbia, Vancouver, BC.

Sears, W. and Sears, M. (2001). *The attachment parenting book*. New York: Little, Brown and Company.

Simon-Kumar, R. (2009). Productive reproducers: The political identity of mothering in contemporary India. *Journal of the Association for Research on Mothering, 11*(2), 143-152.

Simmons, R. (2002). *Odd girl out: The hidden culture of aggression in girls.* New York: Harcourt.

Skinner, B. F. (1953). *Science and Human Behavior.* New York: McMillan.

Smith, D. E. (1993). The standard North American family. *Journal of Family Issues, 14*(1), 50-65.

Spock, B. (1946). *The pocket book of baby and child care.* New York: Pocket Books.

Statistics Canada (2000). *Women in Canada 2000: A gender based statistical report.* (Catalogue 89-503-XPE, 2000).

Statistics Canada (2006). *Employment of Women with Children.* Labour Force Survey.

Statistics Canada (2009). Daycare: The debate over space. CBC News report.

Stoppard, J. M. (1999). Why new perspectives are needed for understanding depression in women. *Canadian Psychology, 40*(2), 79-90.

Stoppard, J. M. (2000). *Understanding depression: Feminist social constructionist perspectives.* New York: Routledge.

Thomas, T. (2000). "You'll become a lioness": African-American women talk about mothering. *Journal of the Association for Research on Mothering, 2*(2), 52-65.

Thurer, S. L. (1994). *The myths of motherhood: How culture reinvents the good mother.* New York: Penguin Books.

Twitchel, J. B. (1999). *Lead us into temptation: The triumph of American materialism.* Chichester, NY: Columbia University Press.

Uttal, L. (1999). Using kin for childcare: Embedment in the socio-economic networks of extended families. *Journal of Marriage and the Family, 61*(4), 845-858.

Vandenbeld Giles, M. (2011). Living in isolation: Motel families in Ontario and the neoliberal social/built/physical environment. *Journal of the Motherhood Initiative for Research and Community Involvement, 2(1),* 194-212.

Walls, J. K. (2010). Implications of intensive mothering beliefs for the well-being of full-time employed mothers of infants: Moderating effects of childcare satisfaction and workplace flexibility. *Dissertation Abstracts International Section A: Humanities and Social Sciences. 71*(6-A), pp. 2006.

Warner, J. (2006). *Perfect madness.* New York: Penguin Books.

Weaver, J. J. and Ussher, J. M. (1997). How motherhood changes life—a discourse analytic study of mothers of young children. *Journal of Reproductive and Infant Psychology, 15,* 51-68.

Weedon, C. (1997). *Feminist practice and poststructuralist theory.* Cambridge, MA: Blackwell Publishers.

White, A. (1950, December 11). Modern woman. *The Globe and Mail,* p. 16.

Weingarten, K. (1995). Radical listening: Challenging cultural beliefs for and about mothers. In K. Weingarten, (Ed.), *Cultural resistance: Challenging beliefs, about men, women, and therapy* (pp. 7-22). New York: Haworth Press.

Wetherell, M. (1995). Romantic discourse and feminist analysis: Interrogating investment, power and desire. In S. Wilkinson and C. Kitzinger (Eds.). *Feminism and Discourse: Psychological Perspectives* (pp. 128-144). London: Sage.

Wives think for selves. (1950, December 6, p. 10). *The Globe and Mail.*

Worrel, J. and Remer, P. (1992). *Feminist perspectives in therapy.* New York: John Wiley.

Wright, S. M. (2000). Educated mothers as a tool for change: Possibilities and constraints. In A. O'Reilly and S. Abbey (Eds.), *Mothers and daughters: Connection, empowerment, and transformation.* Lanham, MD: Rowman and Littlefield.

Wyness, M. (2006). *Childhood and society: An introduction to the society of childhood.* New York: Palgrave MacMillan.

APPENDIX A: TABLE 1
Participant Demographics

Name	Age	Number of Children	Children's Ages	Marital Status	Family Income (All are presenten in Canadian dollars	Paid Employment Status	Ethnicity: Born/raised
Louise	46	2	9yrs./14yrs.	Married	$61,000- $75,0000	Graduate student	British Columbia
Anna	39	2	10yrs./12yrs.	Married	$46,000-$60,000	Professional post secondary, ¾ time	England
Carla	27	1	12 mths.	Common Law	$46,000-$60,000	Graduate student	England
Astrid	30	2	3.5yrs./8 mths.	Married	$31,000-$45,000	Stay-at-home mother	Saskatoon
Aibrean	26	2	7 yrs./5 mths.	Married	$15,000-$30,000	Stay-at-home mother	Rural community in the U.S.A.
Theo	30	1	21 mths.	Married	$46,000-$60,000	Graduate student/ doula/group facilitator	Canadian

Name	Age	Number of Children	Children's Ages	Marital Status	Family Income (All are presenten in Canadian dollars)	Paid Employment Status	Ethnicity: Born/raised
Alice	31	2	7 yrs./3 yrs.	Married	$46,000-$61,000	Stay-at-home mother/ writer	Alberta
Madelaine	36	2	6 yrs./10 yrs.	Married	Over $75,000	Professional, worked from home	Nova Scotia
Lilith	23	2	3 yrs./3 yrs.	Single	$15,000 –$30,000	Student	British Columbia
Jane	37	2	3 yrs./7 mths.	Married	Varies	Professional instructor/ MA student	Ontario/ Raised in various cities around Canada
Catherine	33	1	7 yrs.	Married	Over $75,000	Financial field, full-time	New Brunswick (birth)/ Alberta/ Europe
Alexandra	42	1	8 yrs.	Married	Over $75,000	Management Professional, full-time	Ontario
Nancy	46	3	16 yrs./12 yrs. 8 yrs.	Married	Over $75,000	Self-employed professional, part-time	Quebec
Kate	36	2	4 yrs./6 yrs.	Married	$61,000-$75,000	Community worker, 20 hrs/week, 9 mths/year	Ontario

Dr. Erika Horwitz is a psychologist and the Associate Director of Counselling Services at Simon Fraser University in Vancouver, British Columbia. She is lecturer in the Counselling Psychology Departments at both Simon Fraser University and the University of British Columbia. She has published several articles on the topic of motherhood, and has appeared on television and radio interviews as an expert and advocate for mothers. Dr. Horwitz is a public speaker, writer, and advocate for women's issues. She speaks to women about the current discourse of motherhood with the goal of raising consciousness about the impossibility of the ideal of the perfect mother and to encourage maternal resistance and empowerment. She lives in Vancouver, British Columbia, with her husband, Humberto, and has two grown daughters.